the ebro 1938

death knell of the spanish republic

CHRIS HENRY

the ebro 1938

death knell of the spanish republic

Praeger Illustrated Military History Series

PRAEGER

Westport, Connecticut
London

Library of Congress Cataloging-in-Publication Data

Henry, Chris.
    The Ebro 1938 : death knell of the Spanish Republic / Chris Henry.
      p. cm – (Praeger illustrated military history, ISSN 1547-206X)
    Originally published: Oxford: Osprey, 1999.
    Includes bibliographical references and index.
    ISBN 0-275-98277-7 (alk. paper)
    1. Ebro River, Battle of the, Spain, 1938. I. Title. II. Series.
    DP269.2.E27H46 2004
    946.081'42–dc22 2003063464

British Library Cataloguing in Publication Data is available.

First published in paperback in 1999 by Osprey Publishing Limited, Elms Court,
Chapel Way, Botley, Oxford OX2 9LP. All rights reserved.

Copyright © 2004 by Osprey Publishing Limited

Library of Congress Catalog Card Number: 2003063464
ISBN: 0-275-98277-7
ISSN: 1547-206X

Praeger Publishers, 88 Post Road West, Westport, CT 06881
An imprint of Greenwood Publishing Group, Inc.
www.praeger.com

Printed in China through World Print Ltd.

The paper used in this book complies with the Permanent Paper Standard issued
by the National Information Standards Organization (Z39.48-1984).

10 9 8 7 6 5 4 3 2 1

ILLUSTRATED BY: Adam Hook

CONTENTS

Key to military series symbols

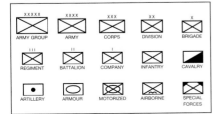

ORIGINS OF THE CAMPAIGN

The he Ebro offensive opened on the evening of 24 July 1938. It marked the final phase of the Spanish Civil War, and to many who had witnessed the previous two years, it seemed as though the conflict could have gone on for ever. In fact, the Ebro was the beginning of the end for the Republican government of Spain. Little did the Prime Minister, Juan Negrín, know that by February 1939 he would find himself addressing the Cortes in a grim castle near Figueras in northern Catalonia for the last time. The Ebro offensive was a final heroic effort carried out by a republic split in two by Nationalist forces and lacking the means to supply its troops. Nevertheless, at the outset it had put the Nationalist army under extreme pressure and only narrowly missed its objectives. The Ebro was arguably the largest Republican attack of the war, and when the *Ejército Popular* was welded into an effective fighting force.

The Spanish Civil War was the product of a number of interactive social and political forces; it would be a simple matter to say that it was a contest between reactionary and progressive ideas, but this is not sufficient. There were broad strands of political ideals which permeated each side, but in reality a soldier could have fought on either side purely because he or she was caught in that zone at the beginning of the war. Families were often split in this way. Equally, they could also be divided by political idealism, which resulted in family members fighting against each other.

The attempted coup d'état which started the war in July 1936 was the culmination of years of distrust between conservative elements in Spanish society and an increasingly aggrieved working class. Under Generals Sanjurjo, Mola, Goded and Quiepo de Llano, uprisings occurred in the major cities in Spain during 17 and 18 July 1936. General Francisco Bahamonde Franco landed in Spanish Morocco on 19 July and immediately took control of the military forces there. The rising was

The River Ebro at the town of Mora del Ebro. This town was one of the only Nationalists garrisons to hold out after the initial attack on July 25. It was surrounded and the 900 men caught inside were finally overcome by the end of the next day by troops of V Republican Corps. (Author's photograph)

intended to put control of the country in the hands of the army. Unfortunately for the conspirators, the plan did not go as expected, and in many areas spontaneous resistance and organised workers' groups put paid to the insurrection, crucially in Madrid and in Barcelona. This was a major blow to the insurgents, or Nationalists as they will henceforth be known. However, in the protectorate of Spanish Morocco they were successful and they managed to get a foothold on the extreme southern tip of the peninsula.

The timely assistance of Germany and Italy in lending aircraft to the fledgling Nationalist cause resulted in the first airlift of troops in history. Moroccan *Regulares* and the Spanish Foreign Legion, the core

THE STRATEGIC SITUATION IN SPAIN PRIOR TO THE EBRO OFFENSIVE, JULY 1938

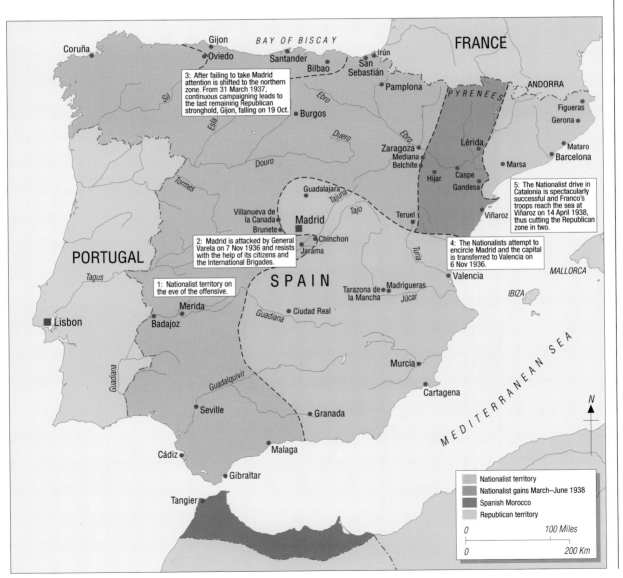

3: After failing to take Madrid attention is shifted to the northern zone. From 31 March 1937, continuous campaigning leads to the last remaining Republican stronghold, Gijon, falling on 19 Oct.

5: The Nationalist drive in Catalonia is spectacularly successful and Franco's troops reach the sea at Viñaroz on 14 April 1938, thus cutting the Republican zone in two.

2: Madrid is attacked by General Varela on 7 Nov 1936 and resists with the help of its citizens and the International Brigades.

4: The Nationalists attempt to encircle Madrid and the capital is transferred to Valencia on 6 Nov 1936.

1: Nationalist territory on the eve of the offensive.

Nationalist territory
Nationalist gains March–June 1938
Spanish Morocco
Republican territory

0   100 Miles

0   200 Km

7

The Fiat CR32, the most
common Nationalist fighter
aircraft of the war. It had a
maximum speed of 354km/hr
and a range of 740km. Its two
12.7mm guns could be changed
for lighter 7.7mm ones if
required. (Museo de Las
Fuerzas Areas)

units of the Army of Africa, allowed General Franco the opportunity to
become a rallying point for those who did not consider themselves part
of the new Popular Front regime. In the north, General Mola was able
to advance towards Madrid from the areas of Castille and Galicia, but
met resistance when he reached the mountains of the Somosierra,
whose passage required control of one of several passes. Mola found
himself unable to advance on Madrid for several reasons: the forces
expected to arise in the capital did not materialise; he had originally
envisaged a force of three divisions to carry out the advance and these
troops simply were not available; and finally the dogged resistance of
left-wing militias. The *ad hoc* units of the Republican militias were not
enough to hold Mola, but continual reinforcements from Madrid
eventually allowed the Republicans time to hold the attackers on the
Madrid side of the passes. Therefore, although the passes of Somosierra
and Alta de Leones fell to the Nationalists, they were held on the other
side of the mountains by the Republicans. The Republican leader Juan
Modesto Guillotte, was heavily involved in these early struggles
commanding the Thaelmann Battalion.

Before long the Army of Africa had swept all before it in a whirlwind
campaign which brought it to the suburbs of Madrid from the south.
The bitter struggle that ensued when General Varela attempted to
assault the suburbs of that city and the prompt arrival of the
International Brigades is a well known story. (A more detailed account
of this stage of the war is available in Osprey's Men-at-Arms 74
The Spanish Civil War 1936–39). As a result of Soviet intervention in
October 1936 and the failure of the workers' militias to fight the Army
of Africa, a new disciplined military organisation was required. This
concept was finally embodied in the Republican Ejército Popular,

which became the main army of the Republic and which fought most of the large campaigns of 1937–39. The transition from militia to regular army caused a great degree of consternation amongst those whose political ideas did not allow them to be controlled by a central government (particularly the anarchists belonging to the CNT, *Confederación National de Trabajo*).

The Nationalists suffered their own organisational problems and certainly their relations with Germany and Italy were not always cordial. By March 1939 Italy had committed over 100,000 troops in phased groups to Spain, mostly Blackshirt divisions, who were not the most effective field troops during the war. The only regular Italian army division employed in Spain was the *Littorio* Division. Regular units were eventually either incorporated into the CTV (*Corpo de Truppe Volontarrie*) or assisted the Nationalist units.

General Varela's repeated attempts to take Madrid were thwarted by the tenacity of the International Brigades, the solidity of its civilian defenders and, not least, by the secret planning of Soviet advisers, who had come to Spain to gain experience and probably to extend Soviet influence in Europe under the premise of the Internationalisation of Socialism. This is not to denigrate the Spanish contribution to war planning, but the general belief among historians is that Soviet advisers were the true thinkers behind the defence of Madrid. The war now developed into a series of attempts to surround Madrid. The battles of the Jarama (5–24 February 1937), Guadalajara (8–18 March 1937) and Brunete (6–26 July 1937) were all attempts to capture Madrid or manoeuvre around the city to gain strategic advantage which would in turn allow its capture. Once it became clear that the capital would not fall (although this was by no means certain during the early attacks), Franco decided that the Nationalist cause would be better served by shifting the emphasis of his assault to the north.

Republican troops leave the Ebro on their advance. The poles carried over their shoulders are probably to help propel the boats across the river. During the retreat Republican troops were able to re-use their bridging equipment and some of the rafts to re-cross the river. (Partido Comunista Española)

The Basque country was an anomaly during this period. Staunchly Catholic and imbued with strong humanitarian morality, the Basque Government had thrown in its lot with the Republic, who had promised them autonomy. Article 1 of the Law statute passed on 1 October 1936 confirmed this. Unfortunately for the Basques, the initial stages of the war isolated them from the rest of the Republic. The fall of Irun on 4 September closed the French border, and it was this large pocket of resistance which the Nationalists decided to eradicate. Since Bilbao, the capital, was the steelmaking centre of Spain and heavy industry was concentrated in the area, the Basque country was an economic as well as a political target. In addition, there were coal mines in Asturias and iron ore in Vizcaya (the province of which Bilbao is capital). The northern front was weakened by the fact that Asturias (the next province) was staunchly revolutionary, socialist and anarchist. The Basques and the Asturian miners made uneasy bedfellows.

After the battle of Guadalajara during March 1937 when an almost exclusively Italian army had been beaten by the Republicans, relations between the Nationalist allies worsened – in fact it has been said that Franco delighted in their discomfiture. However, although the Italians were severely beaten at that battle, the Nationalists still relied upon them heavily for artillery support and weapons.

Although the Soviets were able to supply the Republicans on the northern front with some arms (12 aircraft, 25 armoured cars and other small arms), the northern campaign was an unequal contest. The

The British Battalion of the 15th International Brigade, part of the 35th Division on the Ebro front. In the foreground are the crew of the PM10 Maxim machine-gun which proved effective time and again during this war. (IWM)

Nationalists thought it would be easy to crush this northern pocket, but the Basques proved to be resourceful, and held on at the border of Vizcaya until April 1937. The campaign dragged on until 19 June 1937 when Bilbao fell. The Nationalists' lack of air power was probably part of the reason for this, as protracted bombing campaigns such as the infamous Guernica episode sapped the country's will to resist.

By October 1937 over half of Spain was in Nationalist hands. The last bastion in the north, Gijon, fell on 19 October and Franco had already managed to crush any opposition to his conservative/religious ideas by amalgamating the Falange and Carlist movements earlier in April. On the Republican side, Juan Negrin replaced Largo Caballero as Prime Minister on 17 May and seized the initiative. While the Nationalists attacked in the north, the Battle of Brunete (6–26 July 1937) was the first attempt to relieve pressure upon the Basques by hitting the Nationalists from a different sector. When this offensive became bogged down, a further attempt was made to continue momentum by attacking in Aragon in the Belchite-Quinto sector between 24 August and 15 September. Although these towns were captured, General Kleber, then in command, had little support from the anarchists who predominated on this front, and their uncoordinated attacks again fizzled out with very little gain. Although the Belchite battles had caused some consternation in the Nationalist camp, Franco began to plan again for an attack on either Madrid or in Aragon.

The build-up to the Republican offensive on the Ebro began with the Nationalist drive into Aragon in March 1938. The campaign was intended to follow up the recapture of Teruel and thrust into Catalonia and the Levant (the area around Valencia). An initial armoured thrust was followed by a 60-mile advance in which Republican troops had to fall back from one position to another. The worst nightmare of the Republican command came true when, on 15 April, Navarrese troops arrived at Viñaroz on the Mediterranean. Scenes of victorious troops cavorting in the waves sent shock waves through government circles, who realised that they now had the additional difficulty of trying to communicate across Nationalist lines. President Azaña considered the war to be lost from this point on, although it might have been possible to advance into Catalonia and thus destroy one half of the Republic. Despite a very stiff

The river bend to the west of Amposta where the Republican bridgehead was severely mauled after its initial crossing. Nationalist machine gunners and spotters were positioned along the far bank to impede any crossing attempt. (Author's photograph)

The town of Amposta viewed from the Republican side of the river. This was the southernmost sector of the Republican push. Although much of the area has been rebuilt, scars of the fighting around the town still exist. Resistance to the crossing was stronger in this area as the Nationalists expected an imminent attack. (Author's photograph)

resistance under 'El Campesino'(Valentin Gonzalez) at Lerida, that town had fallen to the Nationalists on 4 April 1938. The way to Barcelona lay open, but Franco hesitated and decided to attack Valencia instead. The direction of the attack was towards the Maestratzgo, that mountainous area extending from south to east, south-west of Tortosa.

The Republican response was vigorous, however, and Prime Minister Negrín has to be given credit for being the backbone of a government which, in many ways, had begun to give up hope. The French border was re-opened on 17 March 1938 after the government of Leon Blum was elected. This meant that large numbers of weapons and supplies could be obtained from a friendly power. Negrin attempted to jolt some kind of diplomatic action by producing his 13-point agenda in May 1938. This speech was intended to draw similarities with policies then in existence in other European countries, but failed to change the political stance of Britain or the United States and therefore, by influence, that of France.

The only remaining path of action, therefore, was a military one. Negrin and the Chief of Staff, General Vincente Rojo, planned a new offensive which would eventually become known as the Ebro offensive.

The canal at Vinallop. Having already crossed the main river Republican troops were forced to attempt a second crossing here but were trapped between the canal and the main river by Nationalist machine guns. They were eventually forced to retire, taking heavy casualties. (Author's photograph)

OPPOSING LEADERS

THE NATIONALIST COMMAND

Agreat deal has been written about Franco; he has been described both as a great hero and a psychopath. Militarily, he does not seem to have had the flair of a Rommel or a Napoleon, but this does not tell the whole story of a man whose personality gives very little away after the passage of so many years. The Germans and Italians criticised his generalship. Mussolini considered him to be intolerably slow in decision-making and was known, according the diaries of his Foreign Minister, Count Ciano, to have derided the delays that were characteristic of the Ebro counter-offensives. Despite other people's criticism, Franco could manoeuvre large armies competently and win decisive engagements, but his long-term aims – the destruction of the Republican armies and the conquering of territory – lead one to believe that he still had many of the qualities of a general of the First World War, and a cautious one at that. Franco's diversion from the Catalonian offensive extended the war for another six months. His obsession with the Alcazar at Toledo, relieved on

General Franco, second left, and his officers on campaign. The figure with his back to the camera is probably General Yagüe, commander of the Moroccan Corps, while General Dávila stands to Franco's left. (Author's collection)

27 September 1936, diverted badly needed forces for the attacks on Madrid. On balance, Franco appears as a leader whose personal intent overrode good military sense, although some modern authors have attempted to explain this reckless caution in terms of the unusual nature of Spanish politics and culture.

General Fidel Dávila was probably one of the most dynamic Nationalist officers and had been involved in planning many of the earlier battles of the war. It was Dávila who declared the state of war during the early days of the uprising. He was to act as Franco's right-hand man during the reconquest of the Ebro pocket and was responsible for many of the direct orders regarding the new offensives.

The commander of the Moroccan Corps on the ground during the Ebro offensive was Juan Yagüe Blanco, a veteran of the 1934 Asturian campaign. Prior to the Ebro offensive Yagüe had fallen foul of Franco (as many people did) for wanting to take a more conciliatory tone with the Republic. As a soldier he was involved in the greater part of the military campaigns of the war and was therefore very experienced. This did not stop him from under-estimating the Republican's surprise attack in July 1937 when he was responsible for stemming the initial assaults.

General Dávila, responsible for the initial declaration of war in July 1936, eventually became Minister of the Army. Dávila took over as the commander of the Northern Army on the death of General Mola on 3 June 1937. He participated in the iron belt campaign around Bilbao in 1937 and was commander during the campaigns of Aragon, the Ebro and Catalonia. (Author's photograph)

THE REPUBLICAN COMMAND

The leaders of the *Agrupación Autonoma del Ebro* were an interesting group in that only one of them, Juan Modesto Guillotte, had any real experience of professional soldiering. Modesto, a *Teniente Coronel* (Lieutenant Colonel) by the beginning of the offensive, had worked as a youth in wine-cellars and a chemist's before enlisting in the army. He was upbraided several times for his lack of discipline, and eventually escaped to Africa where he joined the Foreign Legion, rising to the rank of *Sub-Oficial* (NCO). He joined the Communist party after leaving the Legion and during the Civil War he rose very rapidly through the ranks. Modesto was considered to be one of the ablest military minds of the Republican army, although he was described by his contemporaries as being 'sarcastic, rarely frank, despotic and sometimes brutal'. Nevertheless, he was a leader of ability and proven courage, having fought on the front lines and in almost every main campaign the Republicans had planned.

Enrique Líster, commander of the Republican V Corps, was another matter. He was born in 1907 in Santiago de Compostela and emigrated to Cuba in his youth. On his return to Spain he became politicised and eventually went to the Soviet Union on a political and military course from which, due to his impetuous behaviour, he was excluded and ended up working on the Metro in Moscow instead. Interestingly, Modesto had passed the same course with flying colours. Líster had a stormy relationship with his Communist peers, but he was so able a leader, with a special reputation as a man who would insist upon success in action whatever the cost, that it was impossible to relieve him of command.

Manuel Tagüeña Lacorte worked in concert with Líster and was responsible for command of XV Corps. Tagüeña is an example of a very young man who showed ability and was promoted very quickly through the ranks. The Republican need for officers gave added impetus to speedy promotion. Born in 1913 in Madrid, he had been a leader of Communist students at Madrid University and had been involved in all the combats in and around Madrid. Only 25 years of age at the end of the Ebro offensive, he was a Teniente Coronel.

OPPOSING ARMIES

Historians often compare the Spanish Civil War with one or other of the First or the Second World Wars. In reality it combined distinct elements of both. The heavy artillery barrage and trench mentality look back to the Great War, but armoured assaults and the mass use of aircraft look forward to the Second World War. However, infused with the peculiarly Spanish way of doing things, this war was unlike any others before or after it.

Militarily the 1930s were dominated by ideas of mechanisation and motorisation. The foremost thinkers of the age were divided by the concept of using armoured fighting vehicles in an attempt to force a war of manoeuvre, or of using motor vehicles to make infantry more mobile. At the end of the war in Spain it is obvious that, except in a few cases, the tank was used as an infantry support weapon.

In spite of its later performance in the Second World War, Italy was a force to be reckoned with, and during this period had some very advanced ideas on mechanised units. One American author, J.J.T. Sweet, believes that by the end of the Spanish Civil War the Italians had 'experience in the use of combat tanks, in terms of the number of vehicles involved and their use with infantry troops of their own under their own commanders, something no other country had'. Unfortunately for them, the strain on the economy because of its involvement in Spain effectively curtailed further armoured development after the war.

The Soviet Union had some of its greatest military minds at work in Spain. Both Pavlov and Voronov were considered to be in the forefront of

77mm FK96. A relic of the First World War, this weapon was originally adopted by Germany in 1896 but was widely used in Spain's Civil War by both sides. 100 were supplied to the Nationalists by the Germans in October 1938, but many were already in use having been captured from the Republican forces. (Royal Armouries)

CV33 *Lanzallamas.* This is the flame thrower version of the CV33 tankette, of which several examples were sent to Spain. Although not up to the task of armoured warfare because of poor armament and armour, they were employed as tractors and machine gun carriers right up to the end of the war. (RAC Museum)

military theory, but unfortunately Pavlov and many of his contemporaries were executed during Stalin's purges before their reasoning bore fruit.

On the German side there were early signs that Germany intended to use their armoured force as an attack arm, although claims that the Civil War developed the idea of *blitzkrieg* are highly suspect when one considers that tanks were generally used in the infantry support role. Von Thoma, the Oberstleutnant in charge of Gruppe Imker, the German ground contingent of the Condor Legion, attempted some innovative manoeuvres with the material available to him, but as with the Russians, only a few dubious conclusions were drawn from their combat experience in Spain with armoured formations.

NATIONALIST FORCES

The infantryman was the mainstay of both sides during this conflict. Although the war started off with a mixture of both regular and militia troops, by 1938 the tendency was towards the use of regular units. In this way many of the Christian militia units (*requetes*) had been incorporated into the Nationalist forces, along with those of the Falange, especially after Franco had quashed the disparate political groups under his control in April 1937. The army that defended the banks of the Ebro was from the Moroccan Army Corps and consisted of the 105th Division (one regiment of this unit was left behind on the Levant front) and the 50th Division. In reserve, the 2nd Brigade of the 13th Division was split between the two fronts, as was the 37th Machine-Gun Battalion. The 105th Division also had two battalions of the cavalry division and one tank section.

In terms of morale and experience, the victorious early days of the Army of Africa were over by July 1938. Many of the high quality

ARMY OF THE NORTH

General Davila

MOROCCAN ARMY CORPS

Yagüe

4TH (ALFONSO VEGA), 50TH (COCO) AND 152ND DIVISIONS

ADDITIONAL UNITS:
> One machine-gun battalion

MAESTRAZGO ARMY CORPS

García Valiño

1ST DIVISION

Coronel Mohamed el Mizzian

1ST AGRUPACION – 3 TABORS, 5TH BANDERA OF THE LEGION

2ND AGRUPACION – 3 FET BANDERAS, 7TH BANDERA OF THE TERCIO

3RD AGRUPACION – 2 REQUETE TERCIOS AND 2 REGULAR BATTALIONS
> Two batteries of 65mm cannon
> Two batteries of 105mm guns
> Two batteries of 100mm howitzers

74TH DIVISION

Coronel Arias

1ST, 2ND 3RD AND 4TH MEDIA BRIGADE
> Two batteries of 65mm cannon
> Two batteries of 105mm guns

82ND DIVISION

Coronel Delgado Serrano
> Three batteries of 75mm guns
> Three batteries of 195mm howitzers

84TH DIVISION

Coronel Galera

4 Brigades, each of 3 Battalions
> Two batteries of 100mm howitzer
> Two batteries of 75mm cannon

ADDITIONAL UNITS:
> 53rd Div. (Sueiro) and six batteries of 75mm canon, three 81mm mortar companies, one tank Grupo (Regiment)
> One Foreign Legion Agrupación (artillery Brigade/ ad hoc unit) of tanks (90 vehicles)

CORPS LEVEL ARTILLERY

Moyano
> Eight batteries of 149mm howitzers
> Four batteries of 77mm howitzers
> Two batteries of 75mm field guns
> Two batteries of 155mm howitzers
> Two batteries of 105mm howitzers
> Three batteries of 100mm howitzers

COUNTER–BATTERY UNITS

Castro
> Four 155mm howitzer batteries
> One 149mm cannon battery
> One 155mm cannon battery.
> 260mm mortar Grupo, 210mm howitzer Grupo, 105mm howitzer Grupo, 100mm howitzer Grupo.

Other units were used as the situation required but these have not been highlighted in the original orders.

Moroccan Regulares were dead, and their units had been allocated to various tasks. Inexperienced new recruits from Morocco were simply not of the same calibre. The overall effect of the general expansion of the infantry led to the dilution of its élite units.

The main arm of the infantryman during the conflict was the bolt-action rifle, usually the Mauser M1893 7mm model, or the short carbine version as issued to the pre-war army. It was in general use right up to the end of the war but was supplemented by captured weapons of Czech or Soviet design. The influence of the Germans and Italians meant that many of their weapons were used in the latter part of the war, such as the

Italian Carcano carbine series and the MP-28 sub-machine-gun. Heavier machine-guns were the strip-fed Hotchkiss, the St Etienne M1907, the Maxim M1908 and a variety of captured weapons. A distinct advantage of help from abroad was the standardisation of ammunition and spare parts.

Mortars were used to provide the infantry unit with extra firepower. Many Nationalist weapons were standard German First World War pieces, such as the *granatwerfer* 16 and the 76.2mm *minenwerfer*, although the latter had a tendency to misfire, with disastrous effects.

Before the war Spain had only a few tanks. These were 15 Renault FT17s, organised in three sections of five machines, and one section of five *Verdeja* vehicles, probably altered FT17s. However, the Italians and Germans supplied enough to give the Nationalists a fledgling tank force. The Italians CV33 tankette came in several versions, although its poor armour and fire power meant that by the time of the Ebro offensive it was not commonly used in a combat role. Instead, the Nationalists relied on the Panzer 1 (versions A and B), which was known as the *negrillo*, armed only with two MG34 machine-guns and a maximum of 13mm of armour. These were no match for Republican tanks and anti-tank guns, which inflicted severe losses during 1938. To make up for this deficiency, captured T-26 tanks were incorporated into the Nationalist tank units.

The *Bandera de Carros* of the Foreign Legion was used in the early stages of the battle, organised in six companies of 15 vehicles in three sections. However, combat losses and mechanical failures often reduced numbers and we know that at Villalba de Los Arcos, for example, there were only 12 tanks to a company. In September 1938 the tanks were reorganised once again, this time with three companies to a battalion. The 1st tank Agrupación now had two tank battalions and no longer belonged specifically to the Legion.

Artillery was the arm which eventually gave the Nationalists the edge. Initially Spain was equipped with four main field weapons: the French Schneider M1906 75mm gun; the M1908 70mm mountain gun; the M1919 105mm mountain howitzer; and the M1922 105mm made by Vickers. At the beginning of the war the Nationalists relied entirely on the large amount of Italian equipment available to them. Increasingly, guns such as the 65mm infantry gun M1913, known colloquially as the *tigre* or tiger because of its fierce recoil, came into service. By 1938 about 16 different types of Italian artillery were in use by the CTV or Nationalist troops, ranging from coastal defence guns to anti-aircraft and anti-tank guns. The Germans were more sparing with their equipment, but even so 290 37mm Pak 36 anti-tank guns were supplied to the Nationalists by the end of the war, along with enough Flak 18 88mm guns to form nine batteries, some of which were used at the Ebro counter-offensive. Generally, batteries were of five guns, although this number could change confusingly depending on circumstances. Batteries were then organised into Grupos, often of three batteries. Agrupaciones could be one, two or more Grupos. By the time of the Ebro, batteries were larger than they had been previously, some being of six guns or more.

REPUBLICAN FORCES

The main unit of the Army of the Ebro was the *Brigada Mixta* (Mixed Brigade), a self-contained unit, to be used in different theatres as the basic building block of Republican strength. Theoretically it was supposed to be formed of four infantry battalions, with one artillery Grupo and one anti-tank battery. This neat formation was never really achieved, and during the Ebro offensive most brigades had only three battalions. Again, the number of brigades in a division could vary. For example, on 16 June 1938 the 11th Division was made up of the 100th, 9th and 1st brigades. The breakdown of the total number of men was: 6,628 soldiers, 1,457 corporals, 554 sergeants, three brigade commissars, 13 battalion commissars, seven staff sergeants, seven *alfereces*

Spanish artillery at the Castle of Montjuich in Barcelona. The piece on the left is the Schneider 105mm field gun M1917, the centre piece is the Krupp 15cm K L/45 U-boat gun and the end piece is the Schneider 155/13 M1917. The centre gun is unusual in that its use in Spain was confined to a coastal defence role. (Author's photograph)

Pak 35/36 37mm anti-tank gun was capable of penetrating 38mm of armour at 370 metres. It was also used by both sides as an infantry gun. By the Second World War it had become obsolete. (Author's photograph)

(junior lieutenants), 277 lieutenants, 88 captains and 19 majors. The division also had 92 drivers and 457 additional personnel, a total of 9,602 men.

Their weapons allocation was: 5,739 rifles, 120 automatic rifles, 52 machine-guns, four 81mm mortars, 29 75mm mortars, 51 50mm mortars.

The Autonomous Army of the Ebro was initially formed around 15 April in response to the Nationalist arrival on the Mediterranean

REPUBLICAN ORDER OF BATTLE PRIOR TO THE EBRO OFFENSIVE

SOUTHERN SECTOR

VTH ARMY CORPS

Enrique Líster

11TH DIVISION

Rodriguez

1ST, 9TH AND 100TH BRIGADES

45TH DIVISION

Hans Kahle

12TH, 14TH AND 139TH BRIGADES

46TH DIVISION

'El Campesino' Valentín Gonzalez, then Domenico Leal

10TH, 101ST AND 60TH BRIGADES

ADDITIONAL UNITS
One battalion of the 151st Brigade
2nd Regt. of the 2nd Cavalry Brigade
Two tank companies of the 3rd Tank Battalion and the 3rd Armoured Car Battalion

CROSSING MATÉRIEL

Three pontoon bridges, two lightweight bridges, one heavyweight bridge, one iron bridge and one temporary sluice gate.

CENTRAL SECTOR

XVTH ARMY CORPS

Manuel Tagüeña Lacorte

3RD DIVISION

Cabezos Morente

31ST ,33RD AND 93RD BRIGADES

35TH DIVISION

Mateo Morino

11TH ,13TH AND 15TH BRIGADES

42ND DIVISION

Fernández

ADDITIONAL UNITS:

16th Div. (Mora, this unit belonged to the XIIth Corps), 3rd Cavalry Regt. of the 2nd Bde. two companies of tanks drawn from the 1st and 3rd Bns. (22 vehicles), 1st Armoured Car Bn. and one independent armoured car company.

CROSSING MATÉRIEL

100 boats, five pontoon bridges, two lightweight bridges, one heavyweight wooden bridge, one iron bridge, two flow gates.

35,000 men in total.

RESERVES

27th (Usatorre), 43rd (Beltran) and 60th (Ferrandi), Divs., 7th Cavalry Regt. and two companies of tanks from the Army of the East (22 vehicles in total)

ARTILLERY

XVTH CORPS

Flores

STATIC

150mm battery, 105mm positioned, 107mm positioned, 152mm Grupo positioned.

FIELD:

76mm Grupo, 115mm Grupo and 105mm Grupo

COUNTER-BATTERY:

Two 155mm Grupos, 107mm Grupo

SUPPORT:

Two 77mm Grupos, one 77mm battery, 105mm Grupo.

(Possibly 71 guns in total, not including static pieces)

VTH CORPS

STATIC:

1st ,2nd and 5th Grupos, 90mm coastal guns.
Two batteries 150mm, one battery 150mm howitzers, two batteries of 40mm.

FIELD

Grupo 76mm, Grupo 115mm, Grupo 105mm, Grupo 80mm

COUNTER-BATTERY AND SUPPORT

Grupo 152mm, Grupo 155mm, Grupo 107mm, two batteries of 76mm guns.

There is an exact account of the number of guns ready for use with the Vth Corps dated 23 July 1938. Each Grupo has nine guns and each battery two or three. The total number of guns appears to be 58. In addition, several very old static guns were meant to support the attack where available. These are normally included in the numbers of guns available, but according to the commanders in-situ they were of very little use.

A selection of pistol ammunition showing the wide variety available. From left to right are the Belgian 7.65mm automatic round, French 8mm service revolver, the German 9mm Luger/SMG round, .38 Smith & Wesson, German 9mm Mauser, Austrian 9mm Steyr/SMG, British 450/455 Webley round and the .45 ACP round. (Royal Armouries)

AIR DEFENCE

AGRUPACIÓN 1

GRUPO 3
 three batteries of 76.2mm guns

GRUPO 5
 2 batteries of 40mm guns

GRUPO 9
 4 batteries of 20mm guns

GRUPO 4
 four batteries of 20mm guns

MACHINE GUN COMPANY 61
 6 Gaz trucks with quadruple machine guns.

AGRUPACIÓN 3

GRUPO 1
 3 batteries of 76.2mm guns

GRUPO 8
 2 batteries of 40mm guns

GRUPO 2
 4 batteries of 20mm guns

GRUPO 5
 4 batteries of 20mm guns

MACHINE GUN COMPANY 64
 6 Gaz trucks with quadruple machine guns.

A carriage-mounted Oerlikon 20mm anti-aircraft gun. Two batteries of these weapons were supplied to the Republican 3rd and 35th Divisions for direct infantry anti-aircraft defence purposes. They initially covered the roads leading up to the concentration zone and then were assigned to the Divisions once the crossing had begun. (Museo de Las Fuerzas Areas)

coast to resist any Nationalist attempt to cross the river. Modesto (then a *Mayor*) had Vth Corps at his disposal. The army was expanded by the addition of XV Corps, and around 11 May all its main commanders were promoted to Teniente Coroneles.

Both Republican and Nationalist historians have stated that the Army of the Ebro was in very good condition considering its limitations. Morale was high and the equipment received over the border from France in the previous weeks had served to standardise the ammunition requirement. President Azaña said, 'Almost all of the Army of the Ebro was communist. There is a kind of internal discipline in each unit.' Certainly each unit had its own commissar and this reflected the degree of control which the political leadership had over its men. But Tagüeña stated that many of his men were CNT adherents (anarchists) and therefore it is also true that there were still many disparate political groups within the Republican forces. Desertions were commonplace, but this does not seem to have affected the extraordinary degree of tenacity which many units displayed when defending themselves against the Nationalist attacks towards the end of the campaign.

Despite the losses and incredible hardships which both sides encountered during this campaign, the Republican army was able to retire across the river in good order. We know from a British brigadier's inspection immediately after the collapse of the pocket that sufficient defensive forces were maintained on the other side of the river. Brigadier Molesworth reported on 23–25 November 1939 that, 'The strain of this modern war was shown in the faces of some of these hard-worked staff officers. On the whole, however, they were cheerful with apparently excellent morale.' This officer's staff report (which is part of the PRO collection at Kew) is probing and incisive and the author believes that it is completely genuine.

Equipment procurement for the Republicans was a difficult problem especially during the early period of the war, when weapons were purchased from all over the world. Inevitably this led to a huge variety of ammunition and difficulties of supply. Once the Soviet Union began to supply weapons and advisers (in exchange for large sums of gold bullion) a greater degree of standardisation was achieved in Republican armies. By 1938 this was improved by the brief reopening of the French border.

The Republic relied on many types of small arms, largely the 1891/30 Moisin Nagant 7.62mm rifle, or derivatives of it, and the Czech 7.62mm Mannlicher. Spanish, American and French rifles were all available, but great efforts were made to standardise weapons in individual companies. Sub-machine-guns included the Soviet PPD1934 and some home-manu-

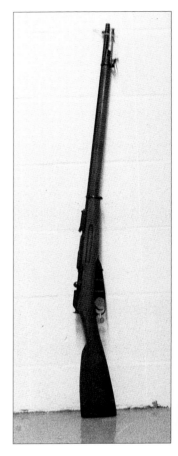

Moisin Nagant 1891/30 rifle. Many versions of this weapon were supplied to the Republicans including earlier Tsarist models and other supplied through shadowy intermediaries. Survivors of the battle have commented that the bayonet needed to remain fixed to keep the rifle aimed on target. (Royal Armouries)

Lanchester submachine-gun copy. This machine-gun was made in the Basque country and for a time small numbers found their way into the hands of the Republican army. By the time of the Ebro offensive small arms were being made from scratch in factories in Barcelona. (Royal Armouries)

factured Lanchester copies. The Degtyyarev DP1928 and the Czech ZB26 medium machine-guns were evident, as were captured Italian Breda Model 30s. The Soviets did not wish to supply their most up-to-date equipment, and therefore donated much old Tsarist or captured German equipment to the Republic. The most frequently photographed machine-gun was the Soviet Maxim PM1910. The use of hand-grenades was common, and after the battle of Guadalajara in 1937 it was said that the Republicans had so many Italian grenades that they were still in use in the Ebro campaign. Since the Italians used their most modern equipment in Spain, they were probably the OTO or Breda Model 35 types, although the French Lafitte types were also common. We know that the Russians delivered quantities of hand-grenades aboard the steamer *Sarkani* on 2 February 1937, but it is not known what kind of grenade they were. A wide variety of pistols were also used. The Spanish Astra, manufactured in Barcelona, was popular, and German Mausers were favoured by both sides.

Other infantry weapons included the German 7.62mm *minenwerfer* supplied to both sides, and the 50mm light mortar. The Soviets supplied a mixed bag of artillery weapons during this period, much of German or British design. The German-designed 77mm Fk96 n.a. was very common, as were many guns manufactured under licence in Russia which were exact copies of British weapons, such as the 4.5 inch howitzer and the 60-pdr., although French and Soviet weapons were also widely used. The 40mm Bofors AA gun is mentioned in several accounts, and it seems probable that these weapons were the main armament of the DCA (*Defensa contra Area*).

In terms of armour, the Soviet-supplied T-26 tank was far superior to anything the Nationalists had. Its 45mm gun was able to destroy any armoured fighting vehicle the Nationalists or their allies possessed. There are records of the BT5 fast tank in Spain, but few of these were supplied and they were used sparingly. Tanks do not seem to have been used to great effect by either side. The quantities of weapons supplied to both sides remains a matter of controversy. There is some evidence to suggest that T-26 tanks or copies were being built in Barcelona, as well as armoured cars, probably the Soviet-designed BA10 or BA6. Some other examples were specially built on a Zis truck chassis. In a visit to the Artillery Park of Barcelona and the Tank School at Granollers on 27–28 November, the previously mentioned British group saw the construction of Soviet T-26s from their constituent parts and the repair of artillery pieces captured during the Ebro offensive. In one officer's opinion, 'The Spanish military authorities [Republican], although they started from scratch have yet succeeded in achieving a production sufficient to render them absolutely independent and to have no need to import foreign supplies.' The problem for the Republicans seems not to have been getting the matériel but being able to supply it to where it was needed.

Republican T-26 tanks on the Ebro front. The heavy camouflage was initially used whilst the tanks had to sit out their wait on the right bank of the river. Olive groves and tree stands kept them hidden from enemy air attack. Many of the vehicles used in the offensive were forced to wait until a bridge or ferry could be constructed with sufficient weight capacity to allow them to cross. (Partido Comunista Española)

OPPOSING PLANS

REPUBLICAN

The strategic aim of the Ebro offensive was to draw off Nationalist forces planning to attack Valencia in the south-central front. Many have since claimed that it was also an attempt to reunite both halves of the divided Republic. Their main aim was successful: the Nationalists were drawn into a bitter four-month campaign that drained their airforce and many of their best units, and it extended the war. There was also a far greater strategic aim for the Republic: to hang on until an inevitable European war developed, when the Republic would be seen as a crucial ally in the fight against the Fascist dictatorships. Indeed, secret Admiralty reports confirmed after the war that Britain may have been better served by supporting the Republic.

The Chief of Staff of Republican forces, General Vincente Rojo, devised the plan which would eventually become the Ebro offensive. However, one highly placed political commissar, Jesus Hernandez, believes that the influence of a Soviet *éminence grise* may have influenced his initial draft.

The Republicans intended to strike at Nationalist communications in Catalonia, especially the important town of Gandesa, which was the

Troops of the International Brigades forming up to go to the front. The lightly equipped troops have reduced any extra baggage to a minimum in an effort to aid mobility and to reduce effort in the intense heat of the day. (IWM)

One of the *puentes de corcho* or *pasarelas*; the light foot bridges used to cross the River Ebro. Hexagonal cork floats were positioned every 2.5 metres along their length for stability. It was theoretically possible to transfer 3,000 men an hour across these constructions. (IWM)

centre of several communications networks. There were two main roads, one from Alcolea del Pinar to Tarragona passing through Mora la Nueva, the second from Gandesa to Tortosa by way of Xerta. In addition, several other secondary roads led to the interior from the town. Therefore the Republicans wanted to create a bridgehead at Gandesa. Not only was the town important for road transport, it was also an important rail hub, as many lines between Madrid and Barcelona and Zaragoza criss-crossed the area. A rapid advance would give the Republicans control, enabling them to connect the two zones.

The final plan of attack was decided at the beginning July in a meeting between Vincente Rojo, Enrique Líster, Sanchez Rodriguez (of the staff of the Ebro Army) and Ruiz Fornells, Chief of the Operations Section of the Central Staff. There were two possible directions of attack: one on the Seros-Fraga-Sariñena axis, and the other on the Gandesa-Valderrobres-Morella axis. The latter was chosen and the order finally issued on 22 July 1938. Since 5 July the Nationalists had been attacking in the Levant but, as ever, the Republicans put up a spirited defence on the line known as XYZ and the Nationalists had suspended their attacks on 24 July.

Rojo held a meeting of senior officers including Modesto and all divisional and corps commanders on the morning of 24 July to confirm final plans. The area from Amposta to Mequinenza would be assaulted, with the intention of carrying out several simultaneous river crossings on a wide front. The main thrust would take place in what was known as the south and central sectors.

The plan would be carried out in four phases. The **main thrust** was to be in the central sector, where one division would cross the River Ebro near Ribarroja and occupy the Sierra de Fatarella. It would probe on its left and seek to link with a second division, which had crossed in the region of Ascó. The axis of march would be the road from Gandesa to Flix. The second division would attempt to occupy the crossroads and Venta de Camposines, and then continue on to Lavall de la Torre and to establish contact with the units of V Corps, to its left, who should be established in the heights of the Sierra de Cabals.

In the southern sector one brigade would cross the river at Benifallet and quickly occupy the heights that dominate the left bank of the River Canaletas and the Sierra de Vallplana, extending to the north-east. Linking with another division of V Corps that would cross at Ginestar, this unit would take as its march direction the road from Gandesa to Tortosa going to Pinell, and then re-entering the Sierra de Cabals and linking on the right with forces of XV Corps. The column which passed Ginestar would employ its forces to surround Mora de Ebro with the aim of cutting the road from Alcolea del Pinar to Tarragona.

Diversionary action in the central sector was to be undertaken by units of the 42nd Division, who would cross the river to the south of Mequinenza and occupy the Auts Hills. They would cut the road from Maella to Fraga towards the north, thus preventing the enemy from creating a bridgehead south of the Ebro in front of Mequinenza. Other units of the same division would cross the river towards the right bank of the River Matarraña to cut the Fayón-Pobla de Masaluca road. In the southern sector a brigade would try to cross the river towards Amposta, cutting the road from Valencia to Barcelona. The intention was to form a bridgehead from which further operations could be carried out.

During the **second phase** the forces that occupied Fatarella in the central sector would advance in the direction of Villalba de Los Arcos-Batea. Those that occupied Venta-de Camposines would continue on the Gandesa-Calaceite and Gandesa-Bot-Horta axes. In the southern sector the occupation of the Sierra de Pandols would be completed after gaining the junction of the River Gandesa with the Canaletas. Secondary objectives in the Mequinenza region were to cover and dominate the right bank of the Ebro and reach Pobla de Masaluca, keeping in close contact with XV Corps.

During the **third phase** the advance in the central sector was to continue to the line Algas-Valderrobres. In the southern sector the advance was to continue along the axis Pinell-Tortosa-Viñaroz, with the right flank in the Sierra de Pandols, where it would link with XV Corps, and from where it would occupy the left bank of the Rivers Mangrané and Serbol. When bridges with heavier weight capacity were constructed, artillery and armour would be transported to the right bank of the river.

The **fourth phase** was simply to pursue the campaign as indicated by the High Command.

These orders are indicative of the complicated nature of the crossing. The plan was studied down to the smallest detail, and every attempt was made to cover potential problems. Small groups of soldiers had infiltrated the Nationalist areas by swimming across the river and noting down areas of troop concentration. Prisoners were taken and interrogated with the same aim in mind. Boats and equipment were hidden in the olive groves and trees near the banks of the river, and vehicles

The River Ebro at Fayón. This was the scene of the stout defence by Nationalists troops of the 7th Battalion of Valladolid during 26 July, their zone of defence extended four kilometres to the south of the confluence with the river Matarraña. (Author's photograph)

were positioned as near to the front as possible without being detected by the enemy.

Engineers and sappers (who were to prove vital as the campaign developed) were distributed between both army corps, but were generally concentrated on the bridges, which were to be built of wood and iron and would carry the heavy matériel.

NATIONALIST

Controversy surrounds the degree of Nationalist preparation for the Republican offensive. It is common for historians to state that although Franco was surprised by the initial crossing and attack, he deliberately allowed the Republicans to extend themselves inland and then cut them off. It should have been a simple matter to surround and destroy them. If this is true then he did not react in a way which would have finished off the Republican army quickly and efficiently. It is clear that the Nationalist high command reacted to events, rather than trying to influence their outcome. The crossing and advance of the Ebro army was carried out in a period of six days which took Republican forces to the gates of Gandesa. It took the Nationalists three-and-a-half months of bitter offensives to recapture the lost ground. And therein lies the answer to the strategic planning of the Nationalists: they were intent on taking ground, and, *poco a poco* (bit by bit), they clawed back Republican gains. No real attempt was made to encircle them, and many of the assaults were virtually head-on attacks. Therefore, claims that all of this had somehow been foreseen tend to ring hollow after the passage of 60 years.

Rumours and intelligence had prepared the Nationalists for the crossing and there is some evidence to suggest that they had significant intelligence of the forces massing across the river and knew their intention. The Italian air force claimed to have monitored the build-up of forces, and a British agent in Burgos reported that the Italian Count Viola de Campaltino claimed that Italian air reconnaissance recorded every detail of the offensive in the course of preparation, and informed General Franco's headquarters. The report goes on to say that this information was ignored, which annoyed the Italians, who had lost many troops in the same area during the Castellon offensive.

Nationalist defences on the right bank consisted of small squads and machine-guns in heavily camouflaged armoured positions surrounded by barbed wire. The possible fording areas were covered by barbed wire, and reserves were kept out of sight wherever possible. Observers, a key component in the plan to alert the Nationalists to a possible threat, were placed in hidden positions near probable crossing points. Yagüe gave orders on 13 July to build concrete blockhouses to reinforce his river line. Considering the vigilance that the Nationalists were supposed to have maintained, it is curious that the Republicans were so successful during the crossing. The Nationalist intention was apparently to hold the line with as little force as possible and then bring up reserves quickly and, if needed, draw other troops to supplement the first line of defence. If this was the case, then it was a complete failure, as will become apparent.

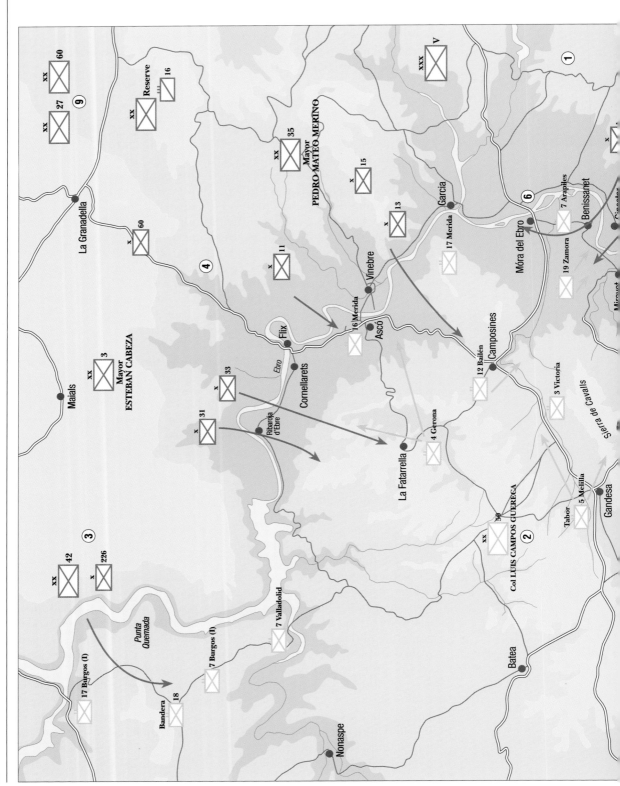

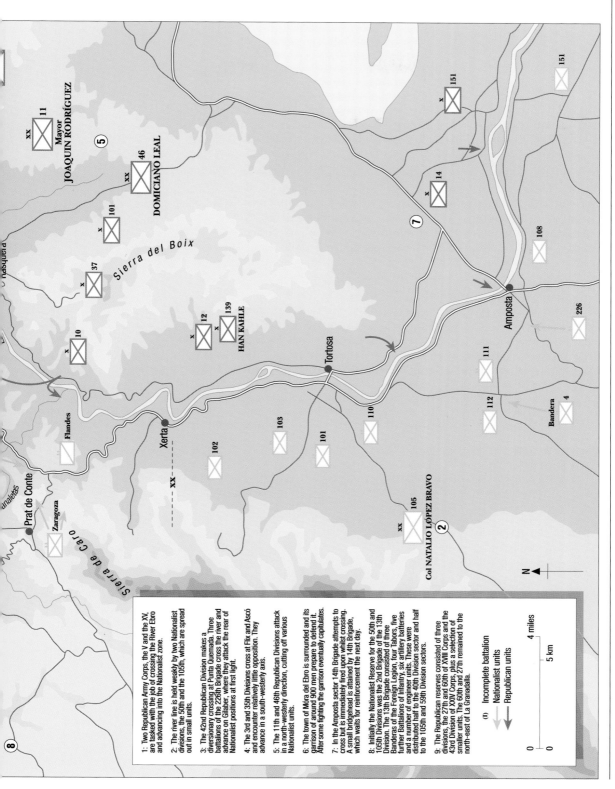

Mayor
JOAQUÍN RODRÍGUEZ

⑤

xx 11

101

46
DOMICIANO LEAL

Sierra del Boix

37

101

14

151

x 151

108

⑦

⑧

10

12
139
HAN KAHLE

Flandes

Prat de Conte

Zaragoza

Sierra de Cano

Xerta

Tortosa

Amposta

226

102

103

101

110

111

112

Bandera
4

105

xx
Col NATALIO LÓPEZ BRAVO

②

N

1: Two Republican Army Corps, the V and the XV, are tasked with the job of crossing the River Ebro and advancing into the Nationalist zone.

2: The river line is held weakly by two Nationalist divisions, the 50th and the 105th, which are spread out in small units.

3: The 42nd Republican Division makes a diversionary crossing at Punta Quemada. Three battalions of the 226th Brigade cross the river and advance on Gilabier, where they attack the rear of Nationalist positions at first light.

4: The 3rd and 35th Divisions cross at Flix and Ascó and encounter relatively little opposition. They advance in a south-westerly axis.

5: The 11th and 46th Republican Divisions attack in a north-westerly direction, cutting off various Nationalist units.

6: The town of Móra del Ebro is surrounded and its garrison of around 900 men prepare to defend it. After some fighting the garrison eventually capitulates.

7: In the Amposta sector 14th Brigade attempts to cross but is immediately fired upon whilst crossing. A small bridgehead is attained by 14th Brigade, which waits for reinforcement the next day.

8: Initially the Nationalist Reserve for the 50th and 105th Divisions was the 2nd Brigade of the 13th Division. The 13th Brigade consisted of three Banderas of the Foreign Legion, four Tabors, five further Battalions of Infantry, six artillery batteries and a number of engineer units. These were distributed half to the 40th Division sector and half to the 105th and 59th Division sectors.

9: The Republican reserves consisted of three divisions, the 27th and 60th of XVIII Corps and the 43rd Division of XXIV Corps, plus a selection of smaller units. The 60th and 27th remained to the north-east of La Granadalla.

① Incomplete battalion

Nationalist units

Republican units

0   5 km

0   4 miles

31

THE CAMPAIGN

The campaign of the Ebro river crossing was the culmination of many different strategic factors. Numerically, it was the largest single campaign of the war and possibly the bloodiest, although sources differ on the casualty rates. It is claimed that 100,000 men took part on the Republican side, but the true figure is probably around 80,000. The range of front stretched from Mequinenza in the north to Tortosa/Amposta in the south, a distance of approximately 70 kilometres. Operations were on a corps/division level rather than battalion/company level. The intention here is to concentrate on smaller actions, many of which were carried out daily over the period July-November 1938.

The River Ebro has been one of Spain's natural obstacles since Roman times. It rises in Cantabria and spreads south-east across Navarre, eventually spilling out into the Ebro delta on the coast near Tortosa. Between Tortosa in the south and Fayón in the north the river spreads in a wide semi circle towards the east. A pair of severe mountain ranges are contained within this bend, the Sierra de Pandols and the Sierra de Cabals, and these would eventually prove to be the key to Republican defence. The mountainous terrain and the numerous crossing points meant that Republican forces would not be so disadvantaged by Nationalist matériel superiority.

Republican soldiers advancing along the railway line, possibly near the village of Bot. All are very lightly equipped. The man second from the left appears only to have an Astra pistol. (Partido Comunista Española)

The river bend at Ascó. The railway tunnel on the right of the picture was used as a staging area safe from enemy air attack. Ascó was initially defended by the Nationalists but was attacked by units of the 11th and 15th Brigades under heavy artillery bombardment. By the middle of the morning of 25 July all Nationalist troops were either dead or had been made prisoner. The ford of Ascó provided the ideal base for a bridge to be built and this was begun as soon as the town had been captured. (Author's photograph)

THE CROSSING AND THE ADVANCE

The night of 24–25 July was dark and the moon gave no hint of the movements of the Republican advance units. At 0015 on 25 July the attack began. The official orders stressed the need for surprise, speed and determination. The intention was not to launch a head-on assault but to infiltrate the Nationalist-held river bank, by-passing areas of strength and getting inland to create a bridgehead. Hundreds of wooden and inflatable boats were silently launched and rowed to the other bank. At the same time several *pasarelas* were positioned – light footbridges on cork floats – which would allow the passage of soldiers in single file across the river. In XV Corps' sector at Ribaroja the machine-gun company of the 121st Battalion were first into the water. In the same zone the 226th Mixed Brigade were in position, while further north the 227th Brigade and elements of the 59th were positioned to carry out the secondary manoeuvre into the Fayón-Mequinenza pocket.

Two battalions of the 226th Brigade crossed the river north of Fayón and continued 15km towards the crossroads between Mequinenza and Maella. They took several hundred prisoners and a battery of 155mm howitzers. A counter-attack was launched the next day by several disparate Nationalist units, one of which was the 18th *Bandera* (Battalion) of the Foreign Legion, who stopped the advance of the 226th Brigade.

The 31st Brigade crossed near Ribaroja relatively easily and made its way to the foothills to the north of the Sierra de Fatarella. The two Nationalist companies of the 16th Burgos nearest to the crossing point put up some resistance but were eventually overcome. The Republicans began to build a footbridge, which was not completed until 8pm. It was attacked eight times by Nationalist aircraft, and when the 3rd Cavalry Regiment attempted to cross, the horses, frightened by enemy bombs,

refused to go on such a narrow causeway. Around 50 horses were killed by bombs, while others fell off the bridge and drowned.

The progress of the 33rd Brigade can be seen from the first bird's eye view. Meanwhile, the 11th International Brigade had started their crossing at Ascó which was opposed by machine-gun fire and went slowly; according to XV Corps' commander. the troops began at 5am, first with small groups of swimmers and then in boats. The Republican artillery responded with artillery fire, and tanks attached to the 35th Division fired from the other river bank. At 7am another light footbridge was begun and three hours later it was completed. Once Ascó was occupied, the Republicans constructed a bridge with a load-bearing capability of 4.5 tons across a ford near the town and, later, Modesto decided to locate his headquarters in the safety of a railway tunnel which ran under the town. Again, air attack was a serious problem, and from 10pm onward air attack was continuous. Enrique Líster said of the attacking Nationalist aircraft, 'The first three days we acted without our own aircraft, conversely the enemy aircraft was above day and night, bombing our troops and matériel with impunity and without interruption'.

The 13th International Brigade carried out a near-faultless crossing on 25 July. The first battalion had crossed by 2am. The battalions quickly headed for Venta de Camposines which was in Republican hands

THE CROSSING OF THE EBRO
24–25 JULY 1938
Republican troops of the 13th Brigade of the 35th Division cross the River Ebro south of Ascó on the morning of 25 July 1938. The initial crossing in this area was lightly opposed by dispersed groups of Nationalist troops. It was carried out by small bodies of soldiers in wooden rowing boats and rubber dinghies. Engineers followed up the first units and assembled *pasarelas*, small footbridges on cork floats, which would increase the crossing rate to 3,000 men per hour. As soon as

the Republicans were ashore they pressed inland in order to penetrate Nationalist territory, avoiding heavy troop concentrations. In this way the 13th Brigade arrived at Venta de Camposines at 0800, capturing Teniente Coronel Peñarredonda of the Nationalist 50th Division before he could clear his command post.

by 8am. Because of this rapid advance, one of the leading officers of the 50th Division, a certain Teniente Coronel Peñarredonda, was captured. From Venta the 13th Brigade headed for Corbera, where the Brigade's concentration of artillery fire and sheer determination eventually crushed Nationalist opposition, which was beginning to form around the 5th *Tabor* (half-battalion) of Regulares and other reserves of the Nationalist 13th Division. Tagüeña noted that a 75mm battery situated on the road between Ascó and Fatarella was repeatedly forced to move its position. The continual threat of capture and involvement meant that the Nationalist guns ended up near Venta de Camposines, where they were captured by the 13th Brigade. By this stage, Nationalist forces were falling back on Gandesa in an attempt to avoid encirclement.

Further south things were not going so well. The 14th Brigade of the

45th Division had three battalions trying to cross at various points: one near the island of Gracía in the middle of the stream, one to the west of Amposta, and the final group near Campredó. Those crossing by the island were met by a hail of gunfire, which holed some of the boats and sank them. Of 100 men, only 40 returned to the left bank of the river. In a similar situation to the west, hand-grenade attacks and machine-gun fire had destroyed the attempt almost immediately. The crossing at Campredó had begun with groups of swimmers armed with hand grenades followed by a wave of boats. This group overcame the defenders and formed a small bridgehead about two kilometres wide between the river and the existing irrigation channel. They were reinforced by groups later in the morning. The difficulty was that in some areas two obstacles had to be negotiated: once over the river the Republicans then had to cross the canal, which runs parallel to it. In many cases soldiers were trapped between the two, unable to cross the canal in the face of stiff opposition. Nevertheless, as Republicans have pointed out, it did tie down the Nationalist 105th Division.

Possibly one of the most important moves came with the crossing of the 11th and 46th Divisions, who occupied Pinell and advanced to occupy the Sierras. Mora del Ebro, with a small garrison of 900 men, had not yet fallen but it was expected to be captured the next day.

The view from the Nationalist side was confused and contradictory, with units reporting *sin novedad* (nothing to report), only minutes before they were attacked. The surprise in many cases was complete. When the true situation dawned on those who were on the receiving end, frantic calls for air support were relayed to headquarters. The Republican command's decision to infiltrate and attack where necessary must have been the correct one. But the response for Nationalist reinforcements was swift, and by mid-morning many units were *en route*. By 10am it became clear that the 105th Division had fared far better than the 50th, who had been scattered between the river and Gandesa. The reports from the Moroccan Army Corps noted that at 9.30am on 25 July orders

The railway tunnel at Ascó, this became the main headquarters for Modesto, head of the Ebro army. In very spartan circumstances, Modesto worked from a table in the tunnel. With only a telephone and his staff around him he co-ordinated Republican advances into Nationalist territory. (Author's photograph)

The key town of Gandesa viewed from Hill 481. This view was taken from between the hills that lie to right side of the road between Gandesa and Tortosa. (Author's photograph)

were given to move regiments and brigades from the 105th, 13th, 82nd and 4th Divisions to cover the disintegration of the front, and this decision included tank units and an artillery Grupo of 77mm guns. Most of these units were to be concentrated initially around Caspe and Ulldecona. It is certain that many of the units that were in line, such as the Vth Battalion of Flandes and the Battalion of San Quintín, were completely destroyed. The net began inevitably to close on Gandesa. Although the whole of the front was in flux, there were two factors that would alter the balance of the advance.

The first happened at about 11.15am when the lock which controlled the flow of the reservoir at Barasona was opened. This increased the volume of water flowing into the River Ebro, raising its level. Secondly, at 10.22am reconnaissance revealed how Republicans were crossing the river. One report stated that there were two light footbridges, one six kilometres north of Amposta and the other a kilometre to the east of Flix. Although this information was incomplete, the Condor Legion was ready to attack and this meant that bombing could now begin in earnest.

At 12.15pm Franco ordered the front to defend the line demarcated by the following points: the Rey summit, Punta Aliga, Corbera, Villalba de Los Arcos, Fayón and Mequinenza, while attempting to link with troops at Xerta. During the afternoon of 25 July Corbera, then defended by Colonel Rubio, was abandoned and the remaining forces under his control fell back upon Gandesa. The Republican foothold in the southern sector around Amposta was finally destroyed at the end of the day by the forces of Coronel Coco. Nationalist losses were purported to

THE FIRST DAY OF THE CROSSING, RIBAROJA–FLIX SECTOR

Viewed from the north-west showing the initial movement of the 33rd Brigade of the 3rd Division across the river and towards Flix. The 60th Brigade are shown along the road from Palma de Ebro, they followed up the 33rd once a light footbridge had been constructed

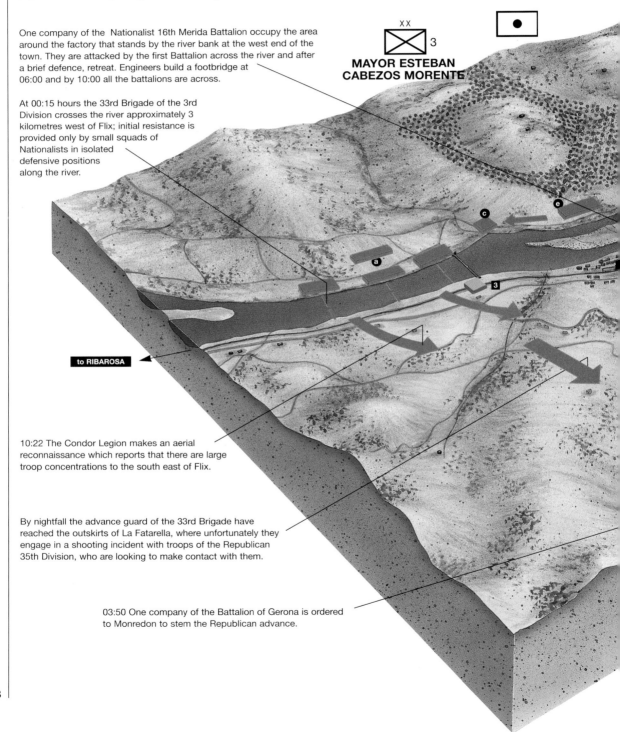

One company of the Nationalist 16th Merida Battalion occupy the area around the factory that stands by the river bank at the west end of the town. They are attacked by the first Battalion across the river and after a brief defence, retreat. Engineers build a footbridge at 06:00 and by 10:00 all the battalions are across.

At 00:15 hours the 33rd Brigade of the 3rd Division crosses the river approximately 3 kilometres west of Flix; initial resistance is provided only by small squads of Nationalists in isolated defensive positions along the river.

MAYOR ESTEBAN CABEZOS MORENTE

to RIBAROSA

10:22 The Condor Legion makes an aerial reconnaissance which reports that there are large troop concentrations to the south east of Flix.

By nightfall the advance guard of the 33rd Brigade have reached the outskirts of La Fatarella, where unfortunately they engage in a shooting incident with troops of the Republican 35th Division, who are looking to make contact with them.

03:50 One company of the Battalion of Gerona is ordered to Monredon to stem the Republican advance.

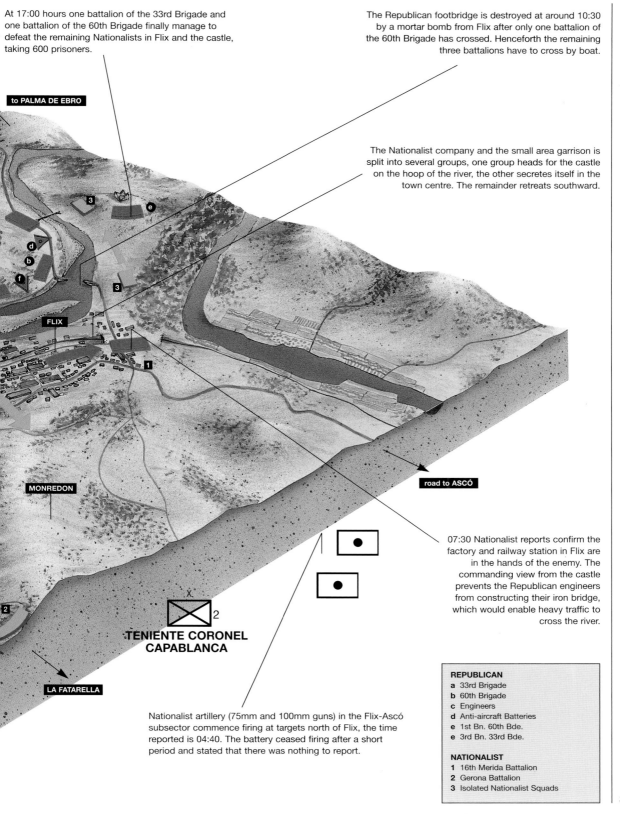

At 17:00 hours one battalion of the 33rd Brigade and one battalion of the 60th Brigade finally manage to defeat the remaining Nationalists in Flix and the castle, taking 600 prisoners.

The Republican footbridge is destroyed at around 10:30 by a mortar bomb from Flix after only one battalion of the 60th Brigade has crossed. Henceforth the remaining three battalions have to cross by boat.

to PALMA DE EBRO

The Nationalist company and the small area garrison is split into several groups, one group heads for the castle on the hoop of the river, the other secretes itself in the town centre. The remainder retreats southward.

FLIX

MONREDON

road to ASCÓ

07:30 Nationalist reports confirm the factory and railway station in Flix are in the hands of the enemy. The commanding view from the castle prevents the Republican engineers from constructing their iron bridge, which would enable heavy traffic to cross the river.

TENIENTE CORONEL CAPABLANCA

LA FATARELLA

Nationalist artillery (75mm and 100mm guns) in the Flix-Ascó subsector commence firing at targets north of Flix, the time reported is 04:40. The battery ceased firing after a short period and stated that there was nothing to report.

REPUBLICAN
a 33rd Brigade
b 60th Brigade
c Engineers
d Anti-aircraft Batteries
e 1st Bn. 60th Bde.
e 3rd Bn. 33rd Bde.

NATIONALIST
1 16th Merida Battalion
2 Gerona Battalion
3 Isolated Nationalist Squads

be 289, but the Republicans no longer had a foothold on the right bank of the river. Furthermore, the Nationalists were able to cover the front from Xerta to the sea.

In the northern area the crossing forces had advanced to occupy the heights of Auts, but the 17th Bandera was defending the Maella road to the south, and two companies of the 17th Burgos Battalion had retreated to Fayón. The stout defence of this town was a disadvantage to the Republicans, because it prevented them linking the two bridgeheads and allowed a later counter-offensive to develop in that area.

The day had ended extremely well for the Republicans; apart from Mora del Ebro, the 70km front, which had been held by the Nationalists, had collapsed. The 35th Division was on the edge of Gandesa, the 3rd was in the Sierra de la Fatarella and the 11th was well established in the Sierra de Pandols. More importantly, the iron bridge at Flix was being completed, as was the wooden bridge at Ascó, both of which would allow the free flow of traffic. In Ginestar and Benifallet wooden *puentes de vanguardia* had been built. Many of the attacks on the Nationalist side of the river were carried out without the support of armour, which could not be transported until heavy bridges had been constructed. At this point Tagüeña, XV Corps' commander, ordered the 16th Division to cross the river, but he was countermanded by General Rojo. With the emphasis on speed, it is difficult to know why this decision was taken but it obviously slowed down the offensive, and this was to have serious consequences.

During the night the Nationalists worked at fever pitch to get reinforcements into the area. Units were drawn from the Central and Levant fronts, while aircraft units moved their bases nearer to the action. One Nationalist fighter pilot, Capitan José Larios, said that his unit had been transferred from Mérida and arrived in battle 48 hours after the first river crossing; one must remember that geographically Mérida is on the other side of the country.

Xerta. From this point south the Nationalists were able to halt the Republican attack across the river. It is obvious from this photograph that the wide river and canal beyond are a formidable obstacle. The troops of the Nationalist 105th Division were able to force the Republicans back, and from relatively early on in the battle the zone from Xerta to the Tortosa remained in Nationalist hands. (Author's photograph)

In addition to the bridge-building capabilities of the Republicans several raft ferries were constructed. Some of them had a weight limit of 30 tons but were used to ferry soft-skinned vehicles and lighter AFV's across the river when the bridges were being used to their capacity. (Partido Comunista Española)

The next day, 26 July, would be crucial for the success or failure of the attack. Although the advance continued, in reality all efforts would be expended on the struggle for the river crossings. As soon as first light illuminated the river valley aircraft were in the air. The lack of Republican air support at this critical stage was strange, and will be examined later.

Many of the armoured vehicles and supply trucks needed on the other side of the river waited at Vinebre, but crossing was severely curtailed at Ascó when a munitions truck ran into one of the support stanchions and severely damaged the bridge. Raft ferries were able to take some of the transport, but the slowness with which the vehicles were able to cross must have been agonising for the commanders. As the morning wore on, successive air attacks began to plague the river crossings. Although there was some anti-aircraft protection, the battle became one of engineers against aviators. If a bridge was damaged by air attack it had to be repaired in the face of further bombing and strafing. To add insult to injury, the opening of flood gates at Tremp and Camarasa meant that the level of the river rose further, causing severe problems for the attackers. The river would continue to rise until 27 July.

THE BATTLE FOR GANDESA

The key to long-term success in this campaign was the capture of Gandesa. In the numerous English language accounts of the International Brigades, great emphasis is placed upon the battle for the town. But there were two army corps sectors in this campaign and the second had as important a role to play in breaking the front. It was the town of Villalba de Los Arcos and the crossroads of Cuatro Caminos, which was to become the focus of the struggle in the central sector.

By the evening of 25 July the Battalion of La Victoria had been ordered to defend Gandesa at all costs. The line of advance was linked by the following points: Republican forces held the heights east of the Pobla de Masaluca and Villalba de Los Arcos. The attackers' line followed the road from Villalba to Gandesa, semi circling the town and passing below it. To the south the summit height of Puig Aliga had been occupied, as had the Sierra de Pandols, an area which would later prove to be a tough nut to crack.

The 13th, 11th and 15th International Brigades were now grouped across the north-east side of the town, some units only 400–500 metres away from the town centre. They were distributed along the part of the

NATIONALIST REACTION TO THE EBRO CROSSINGS
Once the advance of the Army of the Ebro was under way, elements of the Nationalist 50th Division and a tabor of Ifni sharpshooters were forced to escape through the gap left by the 3rd and 35th Divisions of the Republican army. Their route took them straight towards the headquarters of the 13th Brigade at midday on 26 July. Brigade Headquarters was virtually undefended and *en route* they attacked and

captured a Republican armoured car, in addition to a motorcycle dispatch rider who was carrying as his passenger a liaison officer, a Californian called Lieutenant Howard Goddard. Keeping a cool head, Goddard demanded to speak to the highest ranking officer, whom he managed to persuade to surrender his unit. Unknown to the Nationalists it would have been a simple matter to capture both the 13th Brigade Headquarters and possibly that of the 35th, then established at Venta de Camposines.

road from Alcolea to Tarragona, in the heights to the east, and using the dry stream-bed known as Mas de Masserolls as a temporary trench, while the hills bordering the road from Gandesa to Tortosa were under their control. The Nationalist commander of the sector, General Barrón, knew something had to be done quickly if the town was not to fall. Coronel Rubio also had his command post in the town and it was his task to defend the town centre. The local population erected barricades and dug trenches to protect all of the possible access routes into the town centre. General Yagüe sent the 5th Tabor of Melilla to defend the centre. In addition, the 3rd Battalion of Victoria, the 16th Bandera of the Foreign Legion and part of the Tabor Ifni-Sahara were concentrated in

the Gandesa sector. During the night many more units arrived, among them the 1st and 6th Tabors of Melilla, the 6th Bandera of the Foreign Legion and the 4th of the Castillian Falange. At 1.30pm the tank company of the 105th Division set off for the town from the south.

At around 4pm on 26 July the junction between the Vth Tabor and the 3rd Victoria to the north of the town was attacked, and at the same time in the centre Republican tanks began their advance from Cerro de Los Gironenses. There were no real anti-tank gunners on the Nationalist side and the way looked open. But continuous attacks by the 13th Brigade from the north-east, and by the 11th along the Alcolea-Tarragona road during the afternoon, did not gain much ground in the face of an increasingly stiffening defence.

The most serious threat to the success of the Republican attacks came on 27 July. Having established themselves on the summit of Puig de Aliga (Hill 481), Republican forces were subjected to a furious counter-attack by the 6th Bandera of the Legion, who scaled its heights and captured a key position about 2km to the east above the town. The hill is one of the points from which the town can be viewed and tactically gave a great advantage to whichever side held it. There followed a series of Republican counter-attacks in order to re-establish themselves. Descriptions of the attacks on the hill vary, but in the heat of July in Catalonia the Republicans had to assault under fire from the Nationalist

Hill 481, known as *Puig de Aliga* or more pointedly *la colina de muerte* (death hill) by the Republican International Brigadiers. It is viewed from the Nationalist positions. (Author's photograph)

positions at the top. Any visitor to the position today can see that this is almost suicidal and Michael O'Riordon, a member of the 15th International Brigade, commented, 'After the first day's assault they were not only subjected to fire from the hill itself, but also from severe Fascist flank fire on a valley on their right'. One of the most serious problems in the attack on the hill was the almost complete lack of cover for any attacker. Only the shallowest of trenches could be dug and often an assault would falter, forcing the attackers to go to ground caught in a position where they could neither advance or retreat.

The Nationalists also held the position known as Puig Caballé west of the Sierra de Pandols, and because of this the 35th Division, to which the International Brigades belonged, was forced to attempt to encircle Gandesa from the north-east. The 15th Brigade tried to extend its right flank, but every time it did so the Nationalists matched it and reinforced their own flank.

Attacks continued along the front on 28 July, but again it was Puig de Aliga which held the key to the position. The hills around the position

The ridge line of Hill 481. This key height was to prove the final stumbling block for Republican forces advancing on Gandesa. The possession of flanking positions by the Nationalists made this position extremely difficult to overcome. On one side of the hill the slope is gradual whereas on the side where the Republicans attacked it is extremely steep, compounding their attempts to assail it. Today the site has a small iron cross on the summit to mark the spot. (Author's photograph)

THE ASSAULT ON VILLALBA DE LOS ARCOS AND CUATRO CAMINOS

Viewed from the south-east between 26 July and 2 August. XV Republican Army Corps attempts to break the Nationalist line first at Villalba, then at the important crossroads of Cuatro Caminos. This is the furthest advance of XV Corps.

The 131st Battalion of the 33rd Mixed Brigade occupies the cemetery opposite the walled village. The unit has to leave its tank support behind because of damage to the bridge crossing.

Elements of the broken 50th Division, reinforced by the 16th Burgos Battalion and the machine-gun company of the 18th Legion Bandera, defend the houses and walls that line the side of the village opposite the cemetery.

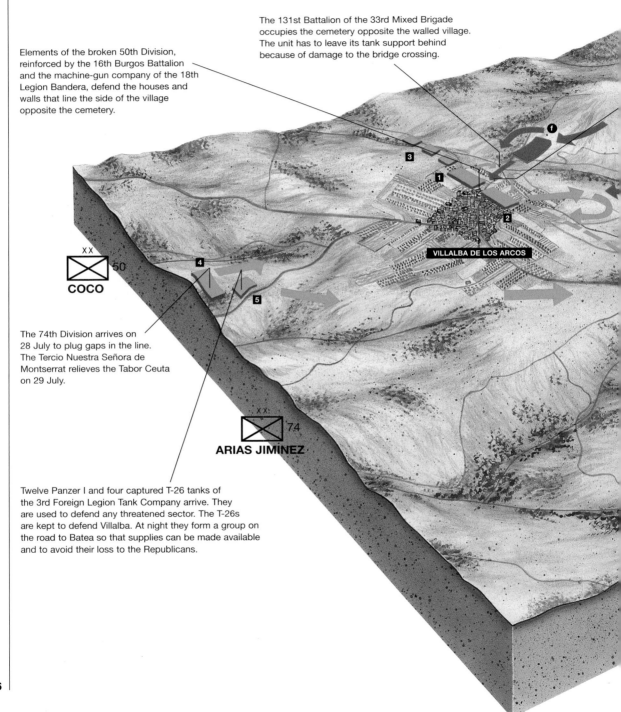

XX
50
COCO

The 74th Division arrives on 28 July to plug gaps in the line. The Tercio Nuestra Señora de Montserrat relieves the Tabor Ceuta on 29 July.

XX
74
ARIAS JIMÍNEZ

VILLALBA DE LOS ARCOS

Twelve Panzer I and four captured T-26 tanks of the 3rd Foreign Legion Tank Company arrive. They are used to defend any threatened sector. The T-26s are kept to defend Villalba. At night they form a group on the road to Batea so that supplies can be made available and to avoid their loss to the Republicans.

The frontal attack on the village begins at 1100 but fails at 1300 due to the height advantage of the defenders and so the attackers retire to the cemetery. Nationalist Teniente Coronel Capablanca, installed within the town, orders a successful counter-attack in which the 18th Bandera and reorganised companies take part. They are supported by machine-gun crossfire, nevertheless the situation remains fluid. A second Republican attack on the evening of the 26th puts the cemetery back in the hands of the attackers and the Nationalists are forced to retreat into the town, where they begin to dig in.

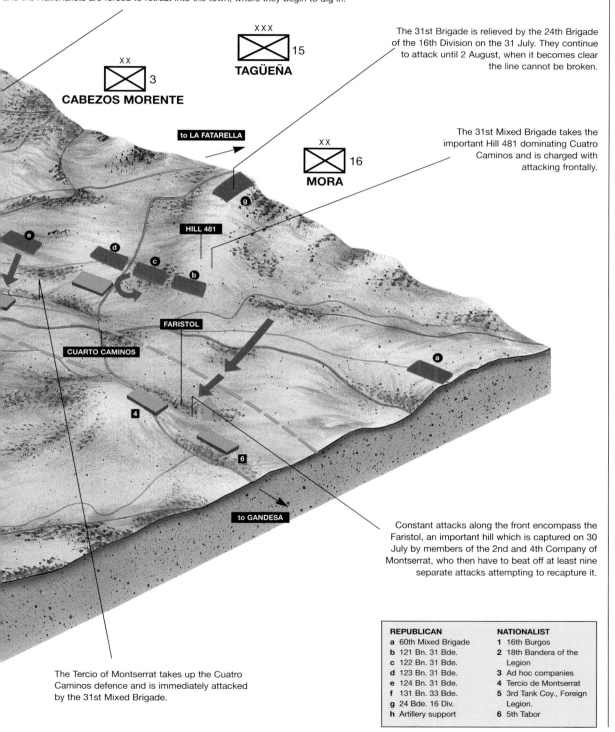

XXX
15
TAGÜEÑA

XX
3
CABEZOS MORENTE

to LA FATARELLA

XX
16
MORA

The 31st Brigade is relieved by the 24th Brigade of the 16th Division on the 31 July. They continue to attack until 2 August, when it becomes clear the line cannot be broken.

The 31st Mixed Brigade takes the important Hill 481 dominating Cuatro Caminos and is charged with attacking frontally.

g

e

d

c

b

HILL 481

FARISTOL

CUARTO CAMINOS

a

4

6

to GANDESA

Constant attacks along the front encompass the Faristol, an important hill which is captured on 30 July by members of the 2nd and 4th Company of Montserrat, who then have to beat off at least nine separate attacks attempting to recapture it.

The Tercio of Montserrat takes up the Cuatro Caminos defence and is immediately attacked by the 31st Mixed Brigade.

REPUBLICAN	NATIONALIST
a 60th Mixed Brigade	**1** 16th Burgos
b 121 Bn. 31 Bde.	**2** 18th Bandera of the
c 122 Bn. 31 Bde.	Legion
d 123 Bn. 31 Bde.	**3** Ad hoc companies
e 124 Bn. 31 Bde.	**4** Tercio de Montserrat
f 131 Bn. 33 Bde.	**5** 3rd Tank Coy., Foreign
g 24 Bde. 16 Div.	Legion.
h Artillery support	**6** 5th Tabor

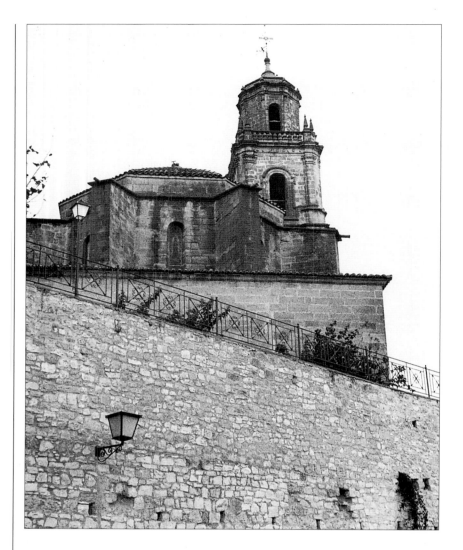

were attacked all day without success. The following day the 16th Division arrived at the front and the 11th Brigade retired to the reserve line. On 30 July the 13th Brigade again attacked to the north of Gandesa, overrunning the road to Tarragona.

At the same time the 23rd and 24th Brigades of the 16th Division made attacks to the right of the line. The cemetery of Gandesa was bombarded by artillery fire and it seemed that this might have been the breakthrough that the Republicans needed, but a Nationalist counter-attack managed to re-establish the original defence lines.

On 30 July, after reorganising the forces at the front, Modesto gave orders for the final assault on the town. This time the operation would be on a grand scale and include two columns, which would encircle the town from north and south. There would now be three groups. Under Tagüeña: the 42nd, 3rd and 60th Divisions (newly arrived from XVIII Corps), as well as the 3rd Cavalry Regiment and two companies of tanks. Artillery support would be two Grupos, plus one battery. The 16th and 35th Divisions, with the 100th and 101st Brigades of the 11th and 46th Divisions under Pedro Mateo Marino, would also include two companies of tanks and two of armoured cars. Four Grupos of artillery were available. Under Líster: V Corps minus the previously mentioned brigades and an additional force of three armoured car and two tank companies. Artillery support would be two Grupos.

Five Grupos would be assigned for counter-battery work. In all, this force would consist of 72 artillery pieces, 22 tanks and 23 armoured cars. However, this figure is probably misleading. Tagüeña, corps commander of XV Corps, stated that the guns were rapidly becoming unrepairable, so this paper organisation may only have been theoretical and the true strength of the forces may have been far less due to casualties and wear and tear.

The plan was to use the 35th Division to fix the Nationalist forces at the front of Gandesa. The 16th Division would pass behind Gandesa and capture key heights to the north-west of the town and then advance along the Alcolea-Tarragona road. Meanwhile, Brigades 100 and 101 would pass to the south-west of the town, cutting the road to Bot and eventually linking up with the 16th Division.

The attacks were carried out on 1 and 2 August, and by this time the Nationalist units of the 82nd and 102nd were on the receiving end. The 13th and 74th Nationalist Divisions were now in line, and they were attacked by tanks. None of these movements produced a significant breakthrough, however, and it may be that Modesto failed to see just how exhausted his troops were after days of intense combat. They were certainly not capable of forcing through an attack

The village of Miravet with its imposing castle on the hill above. At 5am on 25 July Republican troops of the 9th Mixed Brigade crossed here to begin their advance. The castle on the hill was initially by-passed by the attackers but was captured by Republican forces by two o'clock in the afternoon of the same day. (Author's photograph)

in which their opponents became ever stronger while they became weaker.

By 3 August the Republicans had reorganised yet again and since no further gains were possible, the Army of the Ebro went into defensive mode. Franco arrived at the front with his headquarters staff and established his headquarters at Col del Moro, a hill on the road between Alcolea del Pinar and Tarragona. This area eventually served as a site for Dávila and Yagüe as well as other senior staff.

THE ASSAULT ON GANDESA, 26–31 JULY 1938

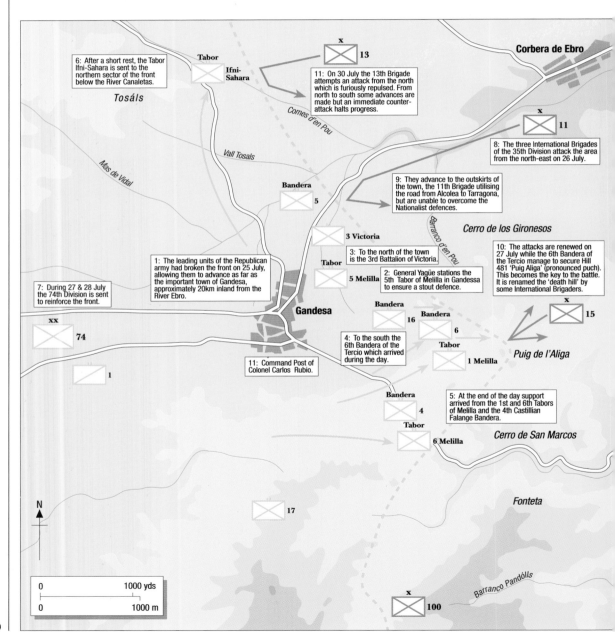

6: After a short rest, the Tabor Ifni-Sahara is sent to the northern sector of the front below the River Canaletas.

11: On 30 July the 13th Brigade attempts an attack from the north which is furiously repulsed. From north to south some advances are made but an immediate counter-attack halts progress.

8: The three International Brigades of the 35th Division attack the area from the north-east on 26 July.

9: They advance to the outskirts of the town, the 11th Brigade utilising the road from Alcolea to Tarragona, but are unable to overcome the Nationalist defences.

1: The leading units of the Republican army had broken the front on 25 July, allowing them to advance as far as the important town of Gandesa, approximately 20km inland from the River Ebro.

3: To the north of the town is the 3rd Battalion of Victoria.

2: General Yagüe stations the 5th Tabor of Melilla in Gandesa to ensure a stout defence.

10: The attacks are renewed on 27 July while the 6th Bandera of the Tercio manage to secure Hill 481 'Puig Aliga' (pronounced puch). This becomes the key to the battle. It is renamed the 'death hill' by some International Brigaders.

7: During 27 & 28 July the 74th Division is sent to reinforce the front.

4: To the south the 6th Bandera of the Tercio which arrived during the day.

11: Command Post of Colonel Carlos Rubio.

5: At the end of the day support arrived from the 1st and 6th Tabors of Melilla and the 4th Castillian Falange Bandera.

Corbera de Ebro

Tosáls

Comes d'en Pou

Vall Tosals

Mas de Vidal

Bandera 5

Cerro de los Gironesos

Barranco d'en Pou

3 Victoria

Tabor

5 Melilla

Gandesa

Bandera 16

Bandera 6

Tabor

1 Melilla

Puig de l'Aliga

15

Bandera 4

Tabor

6 Melilla

Cerro de San Marcos

74

1

17

Fonteta

Tabor Ifni-Sahara

13

11

N

Barranco Pandólls

100

0   1000 yds
0   1000 m

The Spanish Civil War was unique in many ways, it was the first war in which an organised airlift of soldiers was carried out, and it was fought at a time when aircraft and their strategic use – particularly bombing – was a subject of much debate among military planners. From the beginning of the campaign both sides employed a mixture of various aircraft.

In the Nationalist camp the most common fighter was the Fiat CR32 or *chirri* as it was known. Probably the last word in biplane fighter design, it was robust and very manoeuvrable. Armed with two 12.7mm machine-guns, and initially piloted by men of the Italian Reggia Aeronautica, it was provided in large numbers to Nationalist pilots, who were to prove adept at flying it. In all, 405 were sent to Spain. The Italians also relied heavily upon the Savoia-Marchetti SM79 Sparviero the SM81 and some of the Caproni series of bombers. The SM79 was armed with three Breda machine-guns and could carry a bomb load of 1,250 kilos. In comparison, the earlier SM81 had four machine-guns and a bomb capacity of 1,000 kilos. The last two aircraft were found to be particularly robust and able to sustain most punishment from the Republican air force.

General Alfredo Kindelán, head of the Nationalist air forces and the man behind the Nationalist air offensive on the Ebro. Kindelán was initially a Royalist who would have preferred to have King Alfonso XIII on the throne, nevertheless he was very close to Franco throughout the war. Kindelán experienced problems with the Italian and German air contingents, who were disinclined to take orders directly from Spanish officers. (Author's collection)

The German air contingent, the Condor Legion, was equipped mainly with the Heinkel 51 biplane in the early war period. During the Ebro offensive many of these aircraft were replaced by B and C series Messerschmitt 109s. Heinkel 51s were then used in the ground-attack role. In addition, the new JU87A appeared over the Ebro. The bomber complement had also been upgraded, and the majority of aircraft in use were the Heinkel 111B and Dornier Do-17. Many obsolete aircraft were traded to the Nationalists.

Although they started off the war with a very mixed assortment of aircraft, the Republicans came to rely heavily on Soviet machines. Initially the Soviet biplane Polikarpov I-15 (*chato*) dominated the Heinkel 51; it was slower than the CR32, but had better manoeuvrability and it was delivered in large quantities by the Soviets. The most advanced

single-seat fighter of the war was the Polikarpov I-16, which handed air superiority to the Republicans at the end of 1936. Originally earlier versions were equipped with two 7.7mm machine-guns, and, until the arrival of later German monoplanes, it was superior to anything the Nationalists had. The later version, the *supermosca*, was redesigned by Polikarpov in 1937 as the I-16/10 and equipped with four 7.7mm guns. It was this aircraft which was supplied to units on the Ebro front during the campaign.

The twin-engined Tupolev SB-2 bomber was also extremely advanced, and was faster than most of the Nationalist fighters. Nevertheless, the Republican air force was a mixed bag and supply problems severely affected its ability to operate efficiently.

By 1938 the Germans had redressed the technical balance and could field aircraft in large numbers. The cumulative effect was felt when Franco called upon his air force chief, Alfredo Kindelán, to launch an air assault on Republican forces the like of which had never been seen before. Kindelán claims in his memoirs that his orders were to 'destroy and disorganise their deployment, cut their communications with the rearguard and weaken his penetrative capacity'. He was able to marshal around 200 aircraft, which carried out a variety of tasks. The bridges over the Ebro were bombed day and night. Reconnaissance was of the first importance, and a constant stream of information passed back to the high command. As an example, the bombing of the bridge at Ginestar on 26 July severely restricted the flow of vehicles over the river, compelling the attacking forces to act without support from their heavy equipment. The Condor Legion employed the fighter group J-88 and the bomber group K-88 throughout August in the sector. Claims of the success rate are difficult to substantiate, but Francisco Tarrazona, a pilot

Heinkel 111, the main heavy bomber of the Condor Legion during this campaign. The bomb load of 2,000 kilos was effective when used against land defences. Both B-1 and E-1 versions were present in Spain and although initially crewed by Germans, they were eventually used in an all-Spanish group 10-G-25 based in Leon which operated on the Ebro front. (Author's photograph)

in the Republican air force, commented that pilots operating over the Ebro on the Republican side were very young and inexperienced and therefore they lost a high proportion of their aircraft, although he gives no exact figures.

Why, however, during the first three days of the offensive, was there hardly any Republican air support? It would seem that the Nationalists had a free hand in attacking the opposition. We know that Republican fighters appeared over the Ebro in force at the end July and that there were new deliveries of aircraft across the French border in March 1938. This was confirmed by secret Foreign Office reports in Britain, which were based on intelligence from the American Assistant Air Attaché in Paris (previously considered a very reliable source). Some 200 aircraft were available, broken down by the Spanish historian Jesus Salas Larazabal into the following types: 50 I-16s, 50 I-15s and 24 SB-2s. Presumably the remainder were mistaken loads, possibly spares, etc. British sources claimed that 240 aircraft were available on all fronts during this period of the war. The Nationalist air force strength was around 450 aircraft in total.

Garcia Lacalle, the Commander of the Republican Fighter Forces, claimed he had a total of 100 fighters to cover all fronts, due to the attrition rate of the aircraft and pilots. At the time of the offensive only one squadron of Grumman G23 Dolphin ground-attack aircraft was in the area, stationed at Valls, and two squadrons of I-16s – at most 36 aircraft.

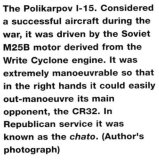

The Polikarpov I-15. Considered a successful aircraft during the war, it was driven by the Soviet M25B motor derived from the Write Cyclone engine. It was extremely manoeuvrable so that in the right hands it could easily out-manoeuvre its main opponent, the CR32. In Republican service it was known as the *chato*. (Author's photograph)

Most of the aircraft were concentrated in the Levant area on the central front to protect the capital, Valencia, against air attack. There were more aircraft available, but many could not be used due to the lack of machine-guns or spares. Considering the amount of equipment needed, air units could be moved relatively quickly to a new base and it seems strange that more machines were not dedicated to the Ebro crossing. Certainly on 30 July Tarrazona was transferred to Vendrell in Catalonia to support the offensive with a force consisting of 12 I-16s and 14 Tupolev SB-2s, but this was a special mission to attack Valderrobles. It was not until 6 August that General Hidalgo Cisneros held a special meeting for pilots who were to fight on the Ebro front. By 7 August there were a total of 70 machines at the front. The following are the *escuadrillas* and their positions on the front: 3rd - Pla de Cabras I-16s (probably the new *supermoscas*);4th - Valls; 6th - Vendrell.

Grupo 26 was formed of I-15s and was distributed between Borjas Blancas, Villafranca del Panadés and Monjos.

The Nationalists used every means at their disposal to attack land and air targets. Particularly successful were the *cadena* squadrons, which were specifically detailed to assault ground targets in a continuous attack by attacking, peeling off and returning behind other members of the group to attack again. This process did not always work, as the Republicans

NATIONALIST REACTION TO THE EBRO CROSSINGS

The first reaction of the Nationalist high command was to divert the majority of its air force to the Ebro front. The immediate intention was to destroy the bridges across the river so that it would be far more hazardous for the Republicans to cross. In addition, the supply lines on the other side of the Ebro could be cut by continuous strafing and bombing. The Duke of Lerma, who flew as a Nationalist fighter pilot during the campaign, commented that the intention, as far as the Nationalists were concerned, was to disrupt Republican rear areas. Therefore all bomber resources were diverted to that aim. In addition, harassing sorties would prevent the reconstruction of bridges. The Nationalists' Italian Fiats relentlessly attacked the bridges at Asco and Flix by using *cadena* (chain) tactics, a flying formation intended to keep a continuous stream of combat aircraft on target. It was the Republican engineers, working continuously under fire, who enabled the Republicans to repair the bridges and therefore keep their supply routes open.

sometimes used dummy vehicles to confuse their attackers. José Larios described one such attack carried out on 8 November which completely fooled his unit.

Estimating the number of aircraft losses on both sides during the Ebro campaign is a futile exercise since the Nationalists claimed to have destroyed over 200 and the Republicans, according to Manuel Azaña, lost around 75 fighters and eight bombers. Whatever the true figure, the Republic lost many aircraft it could ill afford. This may have been down to the youth and inexperience of the most recently recruited pilots. Nevertheless, they were still able to muster a sizeable fighter force to defend the retiring army over the river in November.

The Soviet Polikarpov I-16 supplied in two-gun and four-gun versions by the Soviet Union. The two types were known as the *mosca* (fly) and *supermosca*. On their arrival in Spain in 1936 they were probably the most advanced single-seater fighter in operation in the world and put the Nationalists at a severe disadvantage. (Author's photograph)

STALEMATE: THE SIERRA DE PANDOLS

The early days of August were relatively quiet. The battle for Gandesa had fizzled out and the Republicans were in no position to prosecute their attack further. However, this left both sides in something of a dilemma. Was it possible for the Republicans to defend their bridgehead, and now they had stopped the attack on Valencia, how would the war proceed?

Conversely, the Nationalists now had to deal with a totally new military situation. They were committed on what was effectively a new front. It was now down to them to turn on the offensive, if indeed this was the plan. Considering Franco's previous decisions, this was probably what was going to happen. According to Salgado Araujo, Franco was still concerned with the idea of destroying the Republican army and re-establishing the original front.

There was one very serious problem for the Nationalists: Enrique

Líster's V Corps units were well and truly ensconced in the Sierra de Pandols. This formidable mountain range has a number of peaks over 600 metres high, each a vantage point and observation outpost for the other. With many sheer rock faces and caves, its occupation would be a task for the greatest of military minds. The lack of water in the area would also be a grave problem, the only source being at the Santa Magdalena hermitage positioned high in the hills.

The dispositions of this particular struggle can be seen on the map. The attempt to capture the heights forced the Nationalists to march with their flank exposed to Republican artillery. Once this march was complete, they were expected to ascend Hills 671, 698 and 705 near the hermitage. The initial attempt was an extremely vicious affair, with both sides losing and capturing the heights. The 2nd Flandes Battalion reported that on 10 August they fought for possession of Hill 698 and were attacked constantly from 11am. The position was captured and their report states that the Republicans left around 100 dead in the

THE ATTACK ON THE SIERRA PANDOLS, 9–15 AUGUST

Viewed from the south-west this shows the flank march by units of the 4th Navarrese Division, which intended to attack the line formed by Hills 671, 698 and 705.

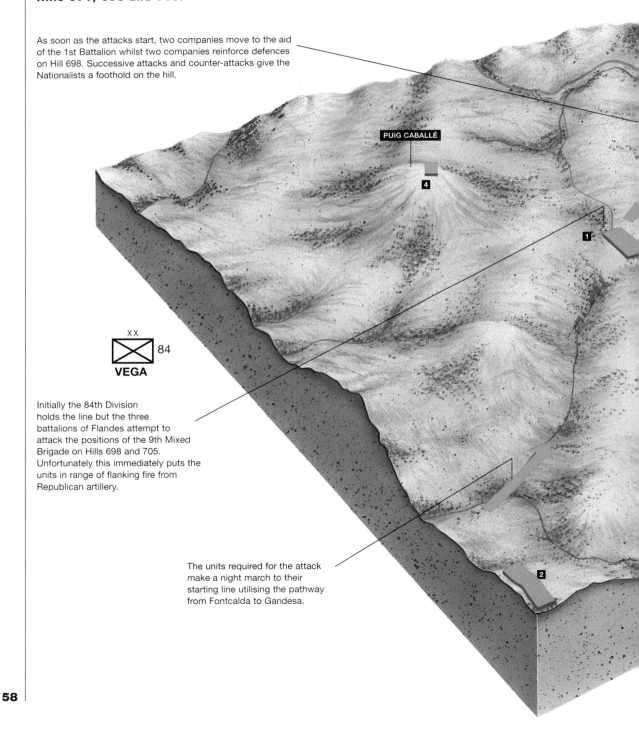

As soon as the attacks start, two companies move to the aid of the 1st Battalion whilst two companies reinforce defences on Hill 698. Successive attacks and counter-attacks give the Nationalists a foothold on the hill.

PUIG CABALLÉ

4

1

X X

84

VEGA

Initially the 84th Division holds the line but the three battalions of Flandes attempt to attack the positions of the 9th Mixed Brigade on Hills 698 and 705. Unfortunately this immediately puts the units in range of flanking fire from Republican artillery.

The units required for the attack make a night march to their starting line utilising the pathway from Fontcalda to Gandesa.

2

On 11 August the Flandes battalions capture the hill and manage on the 12th to position themselves near to Hill 671.

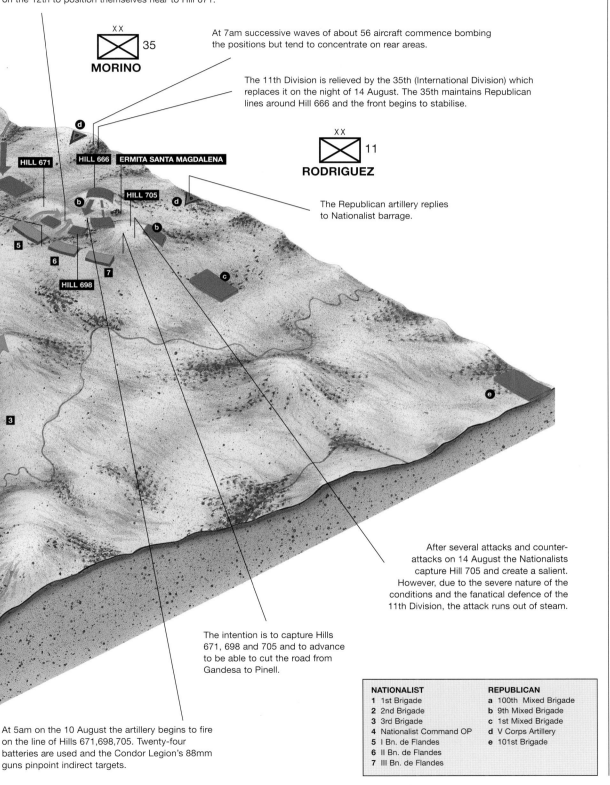

XX 35

MORINO

At 7am successive waves of about 56 aircraft commence bombing the positions but tend to concentrate on rear areas.

The 11th Division is relieved by the 35th (International Division) which replaces it on the night of 14 August. The 35th maintains Republican lines around Hill 666 and the front begins to stabilise.

XX 11

RODRIGUEZ

HILL 671   HILL 666   ERMITA SANTA MAGDALENA

HILL 705

HILL 698

The Republican artillery replies to Nationalist barrage.

After several attacks and counter-attacks on 14 August the Nationalists capture Hill 705 and create a salient. However, due to the severe nature of the conditions and the fanatical defence of the 11th Division, the attack runs out of steam.

The intention is to capture Hills 671, 698 and 705 and to advance to be able to cut the road from Gandesa to Pinell.

At 5am on the 10 August the artillery begins to fire on the line of Hills 671,698,705. Twenty-four batteries are used and the Condor Legion's 88mm guns pinpoint indirect targets.

NATIONALIST	REPUBLICAN
1 1st Brigade	**a** 100th Mixed Brigade
2 2nd Brigade	**b** 9th Mixed Brigade
3 3rd Brigade	**c** 1st Mixed Brigade
4 Nationalist Command OP	**d** V Corps Artillery
5 I Bn. de Flandes	**e** 101st Brigade
6 II Bn. de Flandes	
7 III Bn. de Flandes	

area of the attack. Scenes like these were re-enacted every day. Casualty figures for the Republican defenders were around 50 per cent of divisional strength, and probably higher for the Navarrese Division (to which the battalion belonged) if one takes into account that most of their losses occurred in the Sierra battle. A figure of 7,000 casualties, that is wounded, sick or dead, would not be too extreme. At the end of it the vital Hill 666 still remained in Republican hands, and although the Nationalists had moved forward, the intervention of the 35th Division (International) prevented any further advance. The 4th Navarrese (who had also been supported by three Banderas of the Legion) had been so exhausted by the battles that they were relieved by the 84th Division on 19 August. It took until the early days of November to capture the hill and its defence had resulted in an extremely costly stalemate.

While this battle was raging the Nationalists opened more lock gates on the Ebro to raise the river level again. Between 19 and 21 August three bridges were damaged by the rising levels, further complicating supply problems behind the front lines.

General Dávila, who now commanded the Nationalist Northern Army, wanted the assault to follow a different course. He ordered the Moroccan Army Corps to attempt to break the front at Villalba de Los Arcos, where there had already been fierce fighting. The Republicans were stopped just outside the town. The Nationalists now intended to advance to the important road junction of Cuatro Caminos and then towards the heights of Gaeta, a mountain about three kilometres northeast of Villalba de Los Arcos. This head-on attack, an attempt to smash through to the front, was led by the 74th Division under Coronel Arias Jimenez. He was supported on the left by Delgado Serrano's 82nd Division and on the right by Barrón Ortiz's 13th. The Republicans had the 60th Division (Mayor Buxó) and the 135th Carabiniero Mixed Brigade. The 27th Division (Usatorre) joined them near Hill 444, and in

Villalba cemetery from the Republican side. The village can be seen on the opposite crest. From this point Republican mortars are said to have bombarded Nationalist positions and the cemetery before assaulting and capturing the position. Nationalist troops defended the walls and houses of this side of the village by erecting temporary barricades and blocking off road entry to the town. (Author's photograph)

the rear were the 3rd and 16th Divisions (Cabezos Morente and Mora).

During the recent days of intense conflict, both sides had fortified the ground they had defended. Deeper trenches criss-crossed the area and the position known as Targa was armed with machine-gun points covering all likely directions of attack. The trenches were interconnected and were reinforced by large rocks and covered over with heavy logs.

Before the attack life in this sector was punctuated by the occasional artillery salvo or mortar bomb. A pot-shot might be taken at any of the opposition stupid enough to show their head above the sandbagged parapet. This did not last long, and the Nationalists soon began to concentrate their forces for the next attempt on the line. Troops were brought up to the front line in trucks and then walked to the trenches. All this activity was not lost on the opposition, however hard the Nationalists tried to conceal it.

As usual, the attack opened with the combined fire of 43 batteries of Nationalist artillery dedicated to the task (not including the integral divisional units). The assault began at noon and was led by the 4th Half Brigade of the 74th Division under Cabestré Cardona, which included Battalion B of 131st Bailén Battalion and the Tercio de Nuestra Señora de Montserrat. Neither air attack nor ground attack assaults by unit 1-G-2 (Heinkel 51s) had seriously affected the Republican strong-points, and therefore the classic First World War scenario of trench warfare was repeated. In fact, one of the aircraft was shot down by a member of the Heavy Machine-Gun Company of the 31st Mixed Brigade. The same brigade guarded that front with two rifle companies, two machine-gun sections and a section of 50mm mortars. In addition, there were two tanks and several anti-tank guns in the area which could be used to concentrate fire should the attack materialise. Any tanks intending to go forward with the attackers would also have to contend with hidden foxholes whose occupants had Molotov cocktails ready to turn any tank into a burning metal coffin. The Nationalists actually had three supporting tanks in this sector, but they were quickly forced to retreat in the face of

The *calvario* at Villalba de los Arcos. This building sits on top of a hill which divided the Republican forces from the Nationalists in the village. It was captured by the Republican 131st Battalion and changed hands several times. The position was of great importance to the Nationalists, who had to keep the road from Gandesa open for supplies. (Author's photograph)

the surprise incendiary attacks and anti-tank fire. A tremendous wave of machine-gun and rifle fire trapped the Tercio of Montserrat in their positions from noon until 9pm, when they managed to return to their lines. On this day alone their losses were 58 dead and 170 wounded. In other areas the 135th Carabinieros repulsed three separate attacks on 19 August. The Nationalists gained ground all along the front, however, and by the afternoon of 20 August the 74th Division had moved to outflank Targa, which was captured at 2pm.

The 82nd was the most successful unit: during the three days of combat they had advanced to Hill 527 before Gaeta. These gains did not come easily, however, and the loss of many men took the sting out of the attacking forces. Cumulatively, the ground gained was just three kilometres. Gaeta was finally occupied on 22 August. It had been the command post of Teniente Coronel Tagüeña of the XVth Republican Corps and had an excellent view of the surrounding area. The attacking Nationalists found that it was well defended, but they had been able to encircle the position and pulverise it with artillery and aircraft attacks. Republican forces finally abandoned the site and retreated towards positions that guarded the pass leading to the town of Fatarella. Once Gaeta was captured the Nationalists were unable to advance further. The 74th Division, in the face of stiff opposition, had only been able to advance one kilometre beyond Villalba de Los Arcos.

In some respects this small gain damaged the Nationalists' self-confidence. Disappointed by the lack of decisive success, they began to look in different directions for the key to an attack. Other positions were

In scenes reminiscent of the Great War this photo was probably taken later in the campaign. Note the small shelf for stowing hand-grenades in case of attack. (Partido Comunista Española)

Position Targa. The important position at Cuatro Caminos which dominates the crossroads before Villalba de Los Arcos that the Nationalist Tercio de Montserrat were positioned to attack. This photograph is taken from the right flank of the Republican position and the Nationalist attackers would have come from the right of the picture. (Author's photograph)

taken, but the line continually moved eastwards very slowly. All of this was taking its toll on the Republican defenders, who repeatedly had to reorganise their troops.

The concentration of so much force had been made easier by the operation carried out to the north between Fayón and Mequinenza on 6–7 August. Three separate battle groups had been assigned to eliminate the Republican forces ensconced in the heights of Auts. Reduction of this small bridgehead would allow attacks in the central sector to go ahead without fear of flanking movements by the Republicans. General Juan Vigón was overall commander, while Delgado Serrano controlled troops at the front. Tanks led the attack towards the high ground, but

THE DESTRUCTION OF THE FAYON-MEQUINENZA POCKET, 6–7 AUGUST 1938

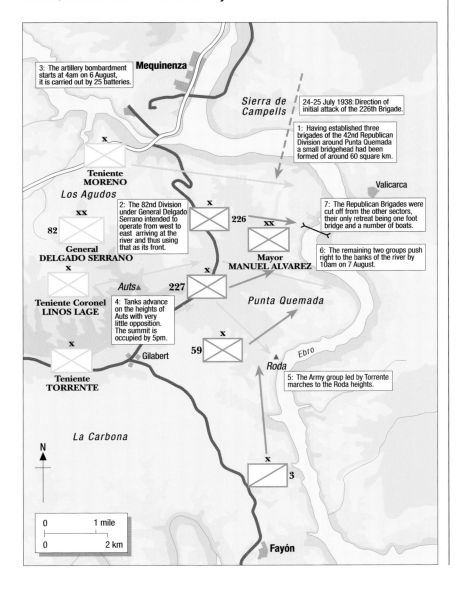

encountered relatively weak opposition, which quickly collapsed, so that on 7 August the Auts had been occupied. The Nationalists took 1,626 prisoners, five anti-tank guns, 40 machine-guns and around 800 rifles, and 817 Republicans were killed. In all, the Nationalists lost around 200 men. Nevertheless, according to the Republican General Rojo, the lesser pocket was never meant to be of much consequence and it had served to distract the Nationalists during the early advance, so that again they had to expend a great deal of effort to recapture the high ground.

The chapel of the Calvario at Villalba de Los Arcos. This building was next to the cemetery, which sat between Nationalist positions in Villalba and those on the other side of the valley. It changed hands several times during the battle for the village. (Author's photograph)

CORBERA, THE SIERRA DE LA VALL AND CAMPOSINES

The next attack was to begin on 3 September, but before it could take place, the Nationalist army was reorganised to incorporate newly arrived units and to give it more flexibility. Two Army Corps were to be formed: the Moroccan under Yagüe and the Maestrazgo under García Valiño. The first corps consisted of the 4th, 50th, 82nd and 152nd Divisions; the second of the 1st, 74th and 84th Divisions. The 13th would remain in reserve, and both corps would have the road from Gandesa to Venta de Camposines as their line of separation. Additionally, artillery fire was increasing daily and the effects of continual air attack began to strain the nerves of the Republicans to the limit. It has been estimated that the Nationalists had more than 350 artillery pieces on this front, and since

Once the Republicans were established in the hills around Auts, defences were built in order to defend the area. This position is one of a number in the area which survive and are built from stone with a deep well to protect the occupants from shrapnel or small arms fire. (Author's photograph)

Franco had organised a general reserve with extra equipment, organisation and supply were greatly improved.

On the Republican side, artillery became more and more unserviceable and ammunition was in increasingly short supply. Although the Barcelona workshops could provide it, the difficulty lay in delivering it to where it was needed.

The Nationalists' capture of the Gaeta peak was not in itself such a great advantage. The valley in the central region which led to Fatarella was heavily wooded and covered in natural obstacles, which made it easy to defend. In fact, the mountain ranges and valleys continued towards the Sierra de Cabals and any new offensive in any direction would not be straightforward. When one considers the combined problems of trench and mountain warfare, the situation appears to be similar to that of the Italians and Austrians on the Isonzo front during the Great War.

The offensive on 3 September was to open with assaults (after artillery attack) by the 1st Navarrese Division in the Sierra Lavall de la Torre and the 13th Division to the north of them. This attack would take place on a narrow front no more than two kilometres wide. The 74th would also attack at the point between the two Republican Corps. The 4th Division was to attack towards the town of Corbera and the net result of this activity would be to capture the town itself. There was to be a second stage: from the heights of Gaeta forces led by the 152nd Division would strike at the 3rd Republican Division, then stationed further north along the mountain path from Corbera to Fatarella. The 27th Republican Division suffered the full force of artillery and air attack. Even the German 88mm Flak 18 guns were used to engage ground targets for lack of suitable air targets, and they proved to be very effective in the indirect fire role, one which is seldom mentioned by later historians, who tend to emphasise the anti-tank uses of the weapon. The 27th could not endure this kind of punishment long, and eventually their right flank began to dissolve. To contain any collapse the 11th Division (considered élite) was rushed to the scene and Modesto ordered it to 'resist without giving a metre'.

Tagüeña attempted to counter-attack to protect XV Corps' left flank. On 5 September the Nationalists occupied Corbera and positions that had threatened Gandesa. The advance units of the 1st Division had been able to capture some of the nearer peaks in the Valle de la Torre and Sierra de

A trench position somewhere in the Sierras, this position has obviously been hastily put up as can be seen from the roof. In many areas no trenches could be dug at all due to the rock base of the mountains. By the time of the first counter-offensives concrete machine-gun posts had been constructed and in many areas there were complex defensive positions. (Partido Comunista Española)

Cabals, but were halted by flanking fire when they tried to advance any further. By 6 September the attackers had ground to a halt, but they had gained important tactical positions. The Sierra de Cabals was imminently threatened and was now the key to the defence of the whole front. In a rapid response to the situation, Modesto ordered the special battalion of machine-gunners to the Cabals peak (of the same name as the Sierra) while the 43rd Division extended their right flank to the northern slopes of the Cabals. The 35th Division was brought into action in the centre of the sector. According to Tagüeña, he then reorganised the army. The 12th Brigade relieved the remnants of the 16th Division occupying Hill 467 south-east of Gaeta. The 16th Division went to the Fayón-Mequinenza sector to replace the 42nd, which had been depleted during 6–7 August. The 60th Division was relieved by the other two brigades of the 45th Division (International, commanded by Hans Kahle), which were then added to XV Corps.

This reorganisation effectively allowed Modesto to control the special reserve battalions and the 45th and 35th Divisions in a counter-attack which, it is claimed,

THE LAST DAY OF THE INTERNATIONAL BRIGADES. **Events in Europe had affected those in Spain. During the negotiations that led to the Munich Agreement in September 1938, both sides promised a withdrawal of foreign volunteers. On the Republican side this meant that the International Brigades would send their foreign volunteers home. Although they intended to leave at an earlier date, they were recalled to the front to respond to a Nationalist offensive in the area of Venta de Camposines on 23**

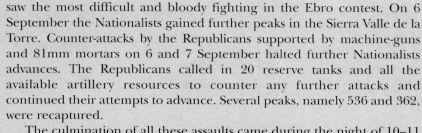

saw the most difficult and bloody fighting in the Ebro contest. On 6 September the Nationalists gained further peaks in the Sierra Valle de la Torre. Counter-attacks by the Republicans supported by machine-guns and 81mm mortars on 6 and 7 September halted further Nationalists advances. The Republicans called in 20 reserve tanks and all the available artillery resources to counter any further attacks and continued their attempts to advance. Several peaks, namely 536 and 362, were recaptured.

The culmination of all these assaults came during the night of 10–11 September. In what has been described as an 'inferno of fire and explosions', the Republicans committed their reserves to prevent any advance into the Sierra de Cabals or further into the line of Valle de la Torre. In total the Nationalists advanced about three to four kilometres on an eight-kilometre-wide front in the direction of Venta de Camposines to the north-east. However, this salient was still very vulnerable since the Republicans still held most of the Sierra de Cabals, which overlooked the Nationalists' right flank. This particular phase of the campaign continued with slight gains on both sides, but without any real tactical advantage being gained. The Nationalists, in spite of their ever increasing material advantage, were not able to cut the Republican supply lines and therefore attacked them piecemeal.

Venta de Camposines, then, was to be the Nationalists' next objective. If the Cabals could not be occupied from the Valle de la Torre, then positions would have to be captured to allow the disposition of artillery which could bombard the area. This was the core of the plan which followed on from the failure of the previous assault. This time, units of the Maestrazgo Army Corps (with the 13th Division) would advance towards Venta de Camposines, while the Moroccan Corps would hold the enemy position. The 74th Division was given the task of neutralising the forces in the Cabals while the attack went ahead. In retrospect, this was not a sensible option. If successful it would extend the salient and leave the Nationalists open to attack from all sides by an enemy who held the high ground. The difficulty of this task is expressed in the 13th Division's official diary, which describes the operations of the 5th and 6th Tabores de Melilla; they had to attack a well-defended Republican position by crossing a gully while being enfiladed by enemy fire. 'The Tabores had to advance clearing the trenches with hand-grenades every ten metres of

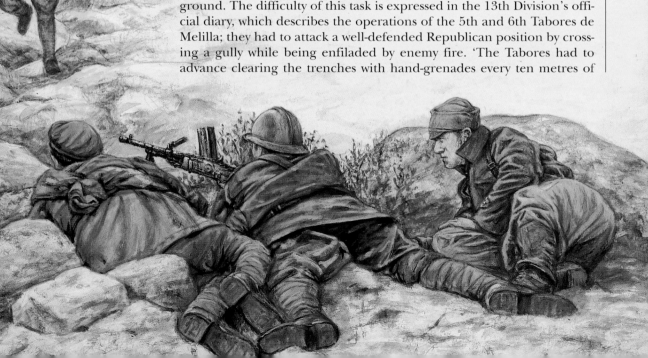

an enemy that had not been destroyed by repeated bombardment or our continuous artillery concentrations'. Two of the most experienced commanders, Capitan Nájera and Comandante Mateu of the 5th Tabor, died on 19 and 20 September. Units tried to work their way along the road from Corbera to Venta de Camposines. During this offensive a trench or defensive position might be assaulted and, unable to capture the area completely, the Nationalists would remove their men and call for air and artillery support to destroy the position.

Meanwhile, political development in Europe had begun to affect events on the Ebro Front. Prime Minister Negrín had attempted a peace settlement brokered by the Duke of Alba at the beginning of September 1938, but it was rejected by Franco. Germany was now preparing for a war over Czechoslovakia, and the Munich Pact ensured a short term peace between the four powers involved, although it completely destroyed any chance of diplomatic redemption for the Republic. Part of the build-up to a diplomatic settlement had been for both sides to agree to the removal of foreign volunteers.

Although there were several international brigades at the front, by the time of their removal they were in reality manned mainly by Spanish soldiers. Unfortunately those who were pulled out were experienced soldiers of the highest calibre who had reached NCO or staff positions. Their removal was to leave some difficult holes in the organisation. Many of these soldiers were in reserve, but their last trial was to come on 23 September when, in order to counter the Nationalist attacks, the Internationals were sent back to the front. The 15th Battalion (British) fought one its hardest battles on that day, only being removed the following evening. It was with great sadness that the Spanish said goodbye to a group of people who had come to Spain for a cause which they

The shallow trenches in the mountain ranges forced soldiers to live a wretched existence. This Nationalist trench is probably somewhere in the Sierra de Cabals but could equally be in the Pandols. Both soldiers are wearing the M1926 Spanish army helmet and to the left of the image ammunition boxes are used for protection. (Anne S.K. Brown Library)

A fact of life during the latter stages of the battle was the reversion to trench warfare in which the hand-grenade was the weapon favoured by the infantry. These Nationalist troops are both using French Lafitte hand-grenades, which were commonly used by both sides during the battle. This scene may have taken place during the struggle for Cuatro Caminos. (Anne S.K. Brown Library)

thought was just. To comply with the negotiations, the Italians sent a token force of troops back to Italy, but given their large commitment, this did not affect the balance of power greatly.

On 2 October Nationalist troops reached the highest peaks of the Sierra La Valle de la Torre; at the same time they were within one kilometre of Camposines. Between 2 and 4 October the 1st and 13th Nationalist Divisions were only able to crawl slowly to their goal. By the end of this particular phase, the 1st Division had suffered a total of 4,612 casualties and it became obvious that these rates could not be sustained. On about 5 October both units were relieved by reinforcements – the

British International Brigade medical units were stationed in a cave near Pinell which acted as a casualty clearing station. This image is Dr. L. Crome of the Medical Mission supervising the setting up of a hospital at the front, probably in the same region. (IWM)

82nd relieved the 1st, and the 53rd the 13th. The 82nd Division continued the offensive between 7 and 12 October, capturing Hill 484 on 12 October which allowed the Nationalist units to cut the road from Fatarella to Camposines. By this stage, both sides were exhausted. The battle had chewed up troops like a meat grinder, and the lack of success

THE FINAL NATIONALIST COUNTER-OFFENSIVE, 30 OCTOBER – 16 NOVEMBER 1938

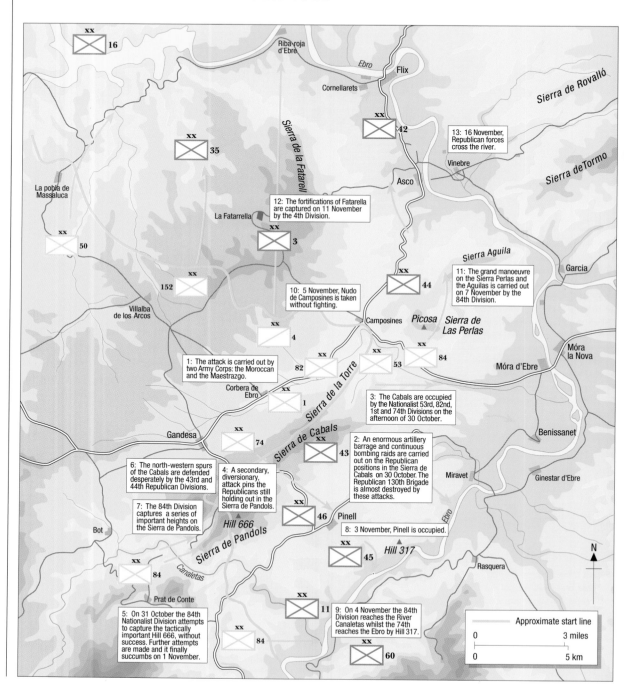

13: 16 November, Republican forces cross the river.

12: The fortifications of Fatarella are captured on 11 November by the 4th Division.

11: The grand manoeuvre on the Sierra Perlas and the Aguilas is carried out on 7 November by the 84th Division.

10: 5 November, Nudo de Camposines is taken without fighting.

1: The attack is carried out by two Army Corps: the Moroccan and the Maestrazgo.

3: The Cabals are occupied by the Nationalist 53rd, 82nd, 1st and 74th Divisions on the afternoon of 30 October.

2: An enormous artillery barrage and continuous bombing raids are carried out on the Republican positions in the Sierra de Cabals on 30 October. The Republican 130th Brigade is almost destroyed by these attacks.

6: The north-western spurs of the Cabals are defended desperately by the 43rd and 44th Republican Divisions.

4: A secondary, diversionary, attack pins the Republicans still holding out in the Sierra de Pandols.

7: The 84th Division captures a series of important heights on the Sierra de Pandols.

8: 3 November, Pinell is occupied.

5: On 31 October the 84th Nationalist Division attempts to capture the tactically important Hill 666, without success. Further attempts are made and it finally succumbs on 1 November.

9: On 4 November the 84th Division reaches the River Canaletas whilst the 74th reaches the Ebro by Hill 317.

Approximate start line

| 0 | 3 miles |
| 0 | 5 km |

N

Riba-roja d'Ebre
Ebro
Flix
Cornellarets
Sierra de Rovalló
La pobla de Massaluca
Sierra de la Fatarell
Vinebre
Sierra de Tormo
Asco
La Fatarrella
Sierra Aguila
Garcia
Villalba de los Arcos
Camposines
Picosa
Sierra de Las Perlas
Móra la Nova
Móra d'Ebre
Corbera de Ebro
Sierra de la Torre
Benissanet
Gandesa
Sierra de Cabals
Miravet
Ginestar d'Ebre
Bot
Hill 666
Sierra de Pandols
Pinell
Hill 317
Rasquera
Canaletas
Prat de Conte

70

brought with it a terrible disillusionment. Nevertheless, the Nationalist high command had further ideas about the direction of attack. The final phase of the long struggle was about to begin.

THE FINAL COUNTER-OFFENSIVE

The key to the front during the last counter-offensive was the capture of the Sierra de Cabals. On 31 August Franco had issued orders to the effect that the Cabals were to be attempted as part of a two-stage manoeuvre. The Nationalist General Garcia-Valiño wrote that the capture of the Sierra de La Valle de la Torre would give the infantry an excellent base from which they could launch an attack on the Cabals. While the attack was being prepared, triumphalist propaganda was used to create an aura of victory for the Nationalists. Huge losses were claimed for their casualty rates and many newspapers reported defeats for the Republicans week after week. As an example of this, the *Correo Español* published in occupied Bilbao on 20 August 1938 claimed 'another great defeat for the Reds on the Ebro', with thousands of casualties on the Republican side.

In reality both sides were suffering great losses, and the continued blocking of Nationalist aspirations on the front was a constant frustration to them. The Nationalist high command met on 23 October to decide on strategy. The thrust of the operation was related by General Dávila the next day, who issued an order to pressurise, pin down and wear out the enemy between Fayón and Camposines and move on the right flank. A secondary attack would be carried out on the remaining position in the Sierra de Pandols, while the main attack would be on the Cabals. This attack would be widened and extended, forcing the Republicans to fall back on the village of Pinell to avoid encirclement. The final position, it was hoped, would be Salvaterras and an arc to the south east of Miravet. The primary assault depended on gaining the heights of the Cabals,

The Sierra de Cabals, a thorn in the side of the Nationalist forces until the very end of the campaign. This mountain range extends from Gandesa east towards Miravet and north-east towards Mora de Ebro. (Author's photograph)

known as the line 631–638, and included the Cabals Mountain itself. A second line would be established after this to protect the left flank. The forces required to carry out the main phase are noted in the order of battle earlier.

The use of artillery would be the key to the success of the whole project. A complicated fire plan and a series of co-ordinated objectives had to be worked out and be flexible enough to allow the choice of target to be changed should the need arise. General Martinez de Campos was in charge of the operation and he had to use not only the divisional artillery, but also that of the Condor Legion and the Italian artillery units under General Manca. In all there were around 500 artillery pieces available for the attack.

Aircraft were also to attack in two phases, firstly to paralyse Republican artillery positions and observation posts in the mountains, secondly to move towards the reserves and their means of supply.

The 43rd Republican Division was positioned in the Cabals. To the north was the 44th Division (transferred from XII Corps), and to the south were the 46th, 11th and 45th Divisions. Northwards from Camposines the 35th and 3rd Divisions defended the front, while the 42nd was in reserve. In addition to this there were independent battalions added to stiffen the divisions in line.

The artillery bombardment began on 30 October and lasted for three hours, initially on a 1½ km-wide front. The calibres of the guns ranged from 75mm to 260mm. According to García Valiño, 175 guns started the bombardment supported by the Italian Legionary complement. Aircraft

Mealtime on the Ebro. This photograph was taken amongst International Brigade troops and shows the wide diversity of uniform used at the front. The variety of headgear is typical of the period. The soldier on the right wears the *pasamontana* cap as do several other men, next to him is an officer with typical hat issued to senior ranks in the Ejercito Popular. The extremely basic cooking facilities were part of everyday life on the front line, where food supplies could be intermittent. (Author's photograph)

The Nationalist counter-offensive on the move. The majority of these troops have Italian items of equipment. The concentration of what appears to be Swarzeloze machine-guns suggests that this units is a heavy machine-gun company. (Anne S.K. Brown Library)

dropped bomb after bomb on the designated targets – some 8,000 tons of bombs were delivered by them and 9,000 tons of artillery shells. The Republican 130th Mixed Brigade, who were the recipients of this storm of fire and steel, lost 70 per cent of their men.

The Nationalist 1st Navarrese Division led the way into the mountains for yet another attempt at the high ground. This time, however, the situation was completely different. Under cover of the terrible bombardment the Nationalists closed right up to their objectives and then began to climb up the last distance before the end of the shelling. In small columns, units of the Foreign Legion and Tabores of Regulares (always relied upon in a crisis) infiltrated and then attacked very specific targets. The weakness of the defence was inevitable after taking such terrible punishment.

In the Pandols things were as difficult as ever – the hills that had given so much trouble, especially Hill 666, were still in the hands of the Republicans, who absolutely refused to give up. Santa Magdalena was

The summit of Hill 671 in the Sierra de Pandols. This mound may have been a strongpoint covering the right of the Republican position. There is still evidence of the fighting left on the top of this position. (Author's photograph)

captured and then lost by the 84th Division. The 74th moved into positions vacated by the 1st Division, while the 82nd captured two heights to its front. By 3 and 4 November, however, nearly all of the areas in the Pandols had either surrendered or been destroyed.

Tagüeña had been sent to Madrid during this attack, and Teniente Coronel Manuel Marquez was covering his post. He arrived back at the front on 2 November to find that the Sierra de Cabals were in the hands of the enemy. Not surprisingly, it was all too much for the severely depleted Republican forces and by the afternoon of 3 November the mountain range which had eluded the Nationalists for so long was in their hands. The Nationalists' special assault groups were supported by divisional machine-gunners, mortar sections and stiffened by the 4th and 6th Mortars Companies.

THE FINAL ARTILLERY BOMBARDMENT OF THE EBRO 24 OCTOBER 1938.
Guns of the Artillery Grupo O.149 commanded by Capitan López Ayala opening fire as part of the Maestrazgo Corps Agrupación. A detailed and extensive fire plan was envisaged to enable an attack to be developed on the right flank in two stages. By the time of this action Franco could mass more than five hundred pieces of artillery to deliver a wave of projectiles at enemy positions. In this case it was the Italian 149mm howitzer that

had been used by the Austro-Hungarian Army in the First World War, which the Italians had received as war booty. In scenes reminiscent of the First World War the Nationalists pulverised selected objectives. Observers on both sides testified that the Republican positions virtually disappeared under a cloud of explosions. The bombardment continued for several hours; for many of the Republican soldiers it appeared they would be consumed under the storm of shells before any other attacks had begun.

The Republican high command now a faced the task of preventing the disintegration of V Corps. The Nationalists were in a strong enough position to push down from the mountains back to the river. According to the original plan, the Maestrazgo Corps were to penetrate and widen their gains. In order to support the Republican defence two extra brigades of V Corps, the 59th and 227th, were included in its forces. Despite this, the town of Pinell fell to a concerted tank and infantry attack by the Nationalist 74th Division on 3 November, and they continued to advance to cut the Gandesa-Tortosa road. By 4 November the 74th Division had reached the banks of the River Ebro near the mouth of the River Cañaletas. Similarly, the 1st Division arrived at the river slightly to the south of Miravet, while the 82nd Division extended towards the final spurs of the Cabals.

Things did not look good for the Republican forces. V Corps sector was now cut in two. In the south, one brigade of the 11th Division and one of the 43rd Division were isolated and so retired across the River Ebro near Benifallet. The 42nd Division defended Miravet, but such was the fluidity of the situation that it had been captured by evening and Nationalist tanks advanced towards Benisanet on 5 November. They began to approach Mora de Ebro and the small mountain range of the Sierra de Picosa. The 60th Mixed Brigade of the 3rd Division and the

Hill 671. To the left of this view one can see a small indentation along the side of the hill, this appears to be the remains of a trench. To the extreme left is Hill 705, which along with this position was the focus of the Nationalist attack in the area. (Author's photograph)

A strange mix of technology and religion, this Panzer I tank is being used as a mobile altar for Nationalist troops before going on the attack. The religious elements amongst the Nationalists were far more prevalent than amongst the Republicans. Despite its obvious inferiority to the Soviet T-26 the vehicle was used throughout the war; attempts to improve its firepower were made by fitting the Breda 20mm 1935 AA gun to its turret. (Anne S.K.Brown Library)

The nature of the terrain on the Ebro. This Nationalist column moves through foothills near the Sierra during the November offensives. (Anne S.K.Brown Library)

226th of the 42nd Division were sent off the Sierra del Aguila in an attempt to hold the front. On 7 November Modesto ordered Tagüeña to take control of V Corps units, presumably as well as his own. Modesto had tried to reorganise the Republican units into three sectors, but this was a thankless task. The units remaining to Líster were either mixed in with XV Corps troops or else had passed back over the river. Tagüeña went immediately to see Líster, who was then at Mora del Ebro, and informed him of this command. Why Líster was not allowed to carry on as commander is not clear and is not evident in his memoirs. Nevertheless, he crossed back over the river on the night of 7 November with all of the V Corps general staff and the 43rd and 46th Divisions.

The Republicans still held a substantial part of the territory in the Sierra del Aguila, however. As for the Nationalists, they could advance northward and attack the XVth in the Sierra de Fatarella if they chose to. This was confirmed by Yagüe's orders to the Moroccan Army Corps on 7 November, whose destinations were to be Flix, Ascó and Ribaroja. Even though the Sierra del Aguila had been heavily fortified, it was relatively easily occupied on 8 November. The fight continued around Camposines and the whole pocket now began to look like a Republican rearguard action. Tagüeña must have known it was now down to him to organise a sound defence and withdrawal. On 9 November he gave orders to retire all artillery to the other bank of the river. The positions at Camposines were encircled by units of the 82nd and 53rd Divisions, and occupied on 11 November. This did not stop the remaining units of the Republican 43rd and 44th Divisions, by now very fragmented, from retreating in good order. In front of Ascó in the north the Republican 42nd Division held a series of fortifications which were meant to be a smaller version of the original bridgehead. Their commander, Manuel Alvarez, was killed by a shell and Modesto ordered Mayor Ortíz to take command of the unit. The 44th Division remained near Fatarella on its eastern foothills. At this time Modesto became involved with a diversionary attack on the River Segre, leaving Tagüeña virtually in charge of the retreat. Fortunately he met the Soviet General Zaponov (apparently by chance) and was able to get him to liaise with Modesto. It is probably only because of Tagüeña's quick thinking that anything of the Ebro army was saved intact. Tagüeña organised a complete plan of retreat which would enable the Republicans to retreat across the river as long as the 42nd Division could hold out until 13 November.

THE ADVANCE INTO THE SIERRA DE CABALS

The Republican commander Manuel Tagüeña Lacorte described the events of the first days of September as one of the most critical moments of the battle of the Ebro. Units of the first Division of the Maestrazgo Army Corps captured the heights between the Sierra de la Vall to the south-east of Corbera and the Sierra de Cabals, specifically between Hills 364 and 551. By using continual artillery and aircraft attacks the Nationalists lay suppressing fire upon the Republican army, who suffered the severest of conditions. The order to resist without losing a metre of ground was given to the Republicans. Inevitably they were forced to use already exhausted divisions to contain the Nationalist advance. The final capture of the heights in the Cabals during October led to the final collapse of the Ebro pocket.

Meanwhile, on 11 November Nationalist General Dávila had Fatarella in his sights. This position was heavily fortified, although it had been little fought over in the previous months and had served as a command post. The attack would be in the direction of Rebasada-Monrédon and would eventually lead to a further advance northwards towards the town of Ribaroja. Six infantry battalions, one tank company and two 65mm *tigre* batteries would be used to advance along the road from Camposines to Fatarella. The two army corps would swing northwards; Maestrazgo to the right heading for Flix and the Moroccan to the left heading north for Ribaroja passing by the Serra peak. This immense manoeuvre was intended to concentrate forces in the Fatarella region, where Republican defenders were apparently still firmly entrenched. In reality, although there were centres of resistance, the Republicans were more concerned with their retreat across the Ebro. The blockhouses and machine-gun points at Fatarella proved difficult, but by this time the Nationalists could avoid areas of resistance and overcome them by encirclement.

The Republican retreat was organised by replacing the 42nd Division with the 33rd Brigade, who had moved from La Gaeta. The 31st Brigade had left their positions at Villalba de Los Arcos to occupy fortifications east of Ascó. The 35th Division retreated to positions east and

The Italian 260mm mortar model 1916, which was a French design by Schneider but was made under licence in Italy by Ansaldo. There were two batteries of these guns (eight in all) situated to the east of Gandesa on October 31 1938. (Anne S.K.Brown Library)

The town of Fatarella, which had been heavily fortified by the Republicans in anticipation of a renewed Nationalist counter-offensive. Although considered to be impregnable by the Nationalists, it was nevertheless captured on 14 November by troops of the 4th Navarrese Division. (Author's photograph)

Illustrating the difficulty of attacking small villages in the region, these small reservoirs at Villalba de los Arcos lie between the hills and the town itself. During the siege of the town the troops of both sides used the small walls and obstacles such as this to inhibit the enemy advance. In addition, the small walled gardens or plots of land (*huertas*) provided an ideal place from which to ambush the attackers. (Author's photograph)

north of Fatarella, arriving at the river next to Ribaroja. The 11th and 15th Brigades were first, with the 13th in reserve on the Monrédon Massif. That night the remnants of the 42nd and 43rd Divisions crossed the footbridge at Ascó. The 44th and 60th Divisions were to retire the night of the 13th in the same place. Interestingly Modesto was still issuing orders, and his last on 14 November urged sustained and tenacious resistance to the enemy. The next day the Nationalists continued to advance but found little contact with the enemy. When they arrived at towns such as Ascó, the Republicans had already moved the majority of their troops across the river. The 4th Nationalist Division arrived near Ribaroja on 15 November, while the 1st occupied Ascó and approached Flix. On the night of 15–16 November the 11th and 15th Brigades crossed near Ribaroja. The last unit to cross were the 13th Brigade, along with headquarters of the 35th Division. Tagüeña and his commissar, Fusimana, went before them. At 4.30pm on 16 November the bridge at Flix was destroyed. Six tanks were transferred by heavy raft ferry and three footbridges were available at Ribaroja, Flix and Ascó, making possible the orderly withdrawal. In fact, Tagüeña stated laconically that there were more means at the army's disposal during their retreat than at the initial crossing! A heavy mist prevented enemy aviators from harassing the operation, and enemy troops were unable to attack the retreating forces. Certainly extra fighter cover was given to the crossings. Tarazona stated that his unit, the 3rd Escuadrilla de Moscas, was sent to protect the river crossings at Flix even in such bad weather. About 40 fighters were sent to cover the crossing. In the event, all passed off in an extremely orderly manner.

The town of Flix viewed from Republican positions on the river. The assault here by the 33rd Brigade led Nationalist defenders to take refuge in the river-side factory or alternatively in the castle, clearly seen here on the top of the hill. At five o'clock in the morning all resistance was overcome and by six o'clock a footbridge was erected. Flix was also chosen as the place to erect a heavier bridge capable of carrying vehicles and artillery. (Author's photograph)

AFTERMATH

After three-and-a-half months of fighting on the Ebro, the greatest battle of the Civil War had come to an end. The immense concentration of troops and men had drained both sides with no territorial gain and in reality very little to show for their efforts.

According to the writer Juan Llarch, the following equipment had been lost by the Republicans during the battle of the Ebro: 18 Soviet tanks were captured and 17 were destroyed, 14 cannon, 29,347 shells, 45 mortars, 213 automatic rifles, 181 machine-guns, 24,114 repeating rifles, 7,635 bayonets, 690 kilograms of explosives, 76,989 mortar rounds, 36,436 hand-grenades, and various other stores. This might seem like an army in full retreat abandoning its arms to the enemy and heading for the safety of the right bank of the river, and yet we know this was not the case. According to the British reports cited earlier, the retreat was orderly and morale, considering the grinding struggle that had just been completed, was relatively good.

Troops returning home from the Ebro front. (IWM)

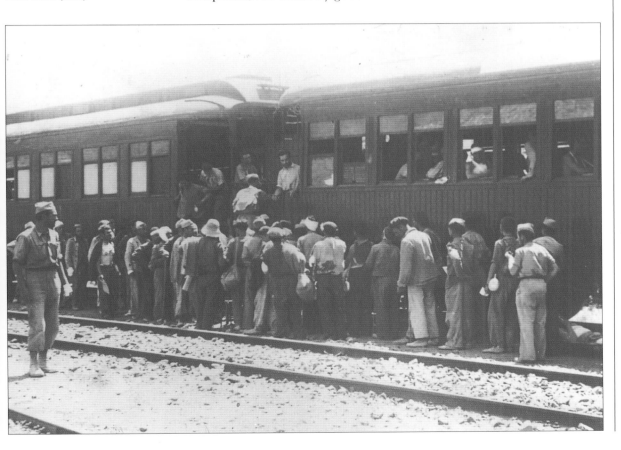

Unfortunately, the Ebro had cost the Republic an enormous amount in terms of casualties and loss of equipment. It is very difficult to calculate the casualties on both sides. Nationalist claims are ridiculously high regarding the Republican figures: Aznar quotes as many as 101,160 casualties. Various attempts have been made to assess the loss – *The Times* calculated the losses at around 40,000 men on each side. It is more likely to have been around this figure, although commanders on both sides have quoted between 50,000 and 60,000 casualties per side.

The original intention of the attack was to draw off National troops converging on Valencia. In that it was successful, but it also drew off a great deal of Republican resources. In addition, the political situation in Europe did not favour the Republic as they had hoped it would. The Munich Pact of September 1938 had (temporarily) put paid to a European war, but it had also shaken the Nationalists, who realised how easy it would be for them to fall in the Czechoslovakian trap. The Nationalist army was severely worn down, as was the Republican and it may be that had this position persisted, a negotiated settlement could have been enforced. Financially, however, the Nationalists were able to trade mining rights to the Germans on 19 November for further supplies of spares and weapons, and this time they were able to launch a devastating attack on Catalonia from Lerida to Tortosa on 23 December. Resistance seemed to be futile, and the whole front collapsed like a house of cards. Most of the population who could flew to France or declared for the Nationalists.

The war dragged on, switching between negotiations and advances. Tarragona fell on 15 January and Barcelona on 26 January. Eventually Colonel Casados negotiated privately in Madrid with Nationalist officers and on 6 March fighting broke out between the Communists and Casados Defence Council in Madrid. Franco would accept only unconditional surrender of the Republic with vague guarantees of safety for those not actively part of the 'Red' regime. It was all over by the end of March 1939. For those who had expected clemency from the victors, life would now enter a new period of repression which was worse in many ways than the war that had preceded it.

THE BATTLEFIELD TODAY

For many people Spain conjures up the image of a sun-drenched beach with gleaming newly built hotels and dark red wines. This is obviously only one side of the country's rich and varied cultural heritage, and the region in which this campaign took place is very rarely visited by the tourist. It can be reached relatively easily by driving out from Barcelona to Tortosa on the coast road. Any turning inland to Zaragossa or heading towards Madrid will take you into the area. To see the full extent of the battle the traveller will need a car. Public transport is sporadic and goes nowhere near some of the obscure places of the battle.

Catalonia is a rich agricultural area, although it also has an advanced technologically aware business community, especially in Barcelona. The activities of the small towns in the region tend towards vineyards or olive growing. In summer it is intensely hot, while in winter it rains a great deal. Any visitor to the region in summer will appreciate what it must have been like to have to fight a campaign often with no shade and the

The bridge at Bot still retains scars of the fighting in this area. The town lies to the south-west of Gandesa and proved to be an important transit centre for Nationalist troops on their way to fight in the Sierra de Pandols. (Author's photograph)

The Nationalist War Memorial in Tortosa. This huge object rises up in the middle of the River Ebro and is easily found if one follows the riverside into the town. (Author's photograph)

only protection that of the olive trees or small walls.

Gandesa is now a small commercial centre and a good place to stay in the area; the famous Hill 481 is located just outside the town and can be reached off the Gandesa to Tortosa road. Its summit is marked with a small cross. Climbing this hill gives a very good impression of the overall terrain and underlines the importance of this feature in the capture of the town.

The battle was fought only 60 years ago but very little remains of the defensive systems built by both sides. Unlike battles that took place before the 20th century where the distances were small, the Ebro offensive covered a large area, the movement was fluid, and the battlefields in the Sierras were, until very recently, inaccessible. One can visit the small towns such as Ascó, Flix, Amposta along the river to gain an idea of the scale of the logistical problems. Very occasionally one comes across a bullet-splattered house or bridge. In Ascó the railway tunnel where Modesto had his headquarters is still as it was. The hills around La Fatarella still show some signs of defensive construction, although many of the concrete pill boxes have been destroyed. The village of Villalba de Los Arcos is almost exactly as it was during the war, although new roads have been constructed. One can visit the small chapel and the cemetery, which was lost and captured by both sides during the early part of the conflict.

There are several large monuments to the dead of the battle and these tend to be in memory of Nationalist units since they were the victors. In Tortosa there is a huge monument to the dead and in many of the more intensely fought battle areas there are monuments to various units. Cuatro Caminos where the dedication is to the Tercio de Nuestra Señora de Montserrat is notable.

The mountains of the area are natural phenomena of great beauty. It is possible to take a car off-road to follow the tracks into the hills, but a four-wheel-drive vehicle would be an advantage. The hermitage of Santa Magdalena – the centre of Republican resistance in the Pandols – can be reached by car relatively easily. If one has a good map, it is possible to work out which of the peaks were contested, although virtually all of them in the surrounding area were fought over at one stage or other. It is more difficult to travel in the Sierra de Cabals, but with a good map it is possible to hike into the region.

CHRONOLOGY

5 April 1938 Negrín takes over as War Minister after sacking the previous post-holder, Indalecio Prieto.

14 April Nationalists reach Viñaroz; the Republic now has to operate in two separate zones.

20 April Nationalists attempt to attack Valencia.

29 and 30 April Beginning of reorganisation of Republican units in Catalonia. The Army of the Ebro is conceived.

20–23 July Successful defence of XYZ line in the Levant by Republican forces.

24–25 July The Nationalists cross the Ebro and the offensive begins.

26–31 July Battle for Gandesa. The assault and defence of Villalba de Los Arcos.

30 July – 2 August Main assault on Cuatro Caminos; lesser attacks continue afterwards.

1 August Army of the Ebro ordered to go on the defensive.

6–7 August Destruction of the Fayón-Mequinenza pocket.

9–19 August Nationalist assault on the Sierra de Pandols.

3–13 September Assaults on Corbera and the Sierra de la Vall; failure by the Nationalists to enter Sierra de Cabals.

18 September – 14 October Battle of Camposines.

23 September International Brigades' last battle.

30 September Munich Pact signed by Britain, France, Italy and Germany, thus altering the balance of power in Europe unfavourably for the Republic.

1 October Negrín announces new organisation of Republican army. Two army groups: six armies of variable size and 23 army corps of the same composition.

30 October – 14 November Final Nationalist counter-offensive.

16 November Last units of Army of the Ebro retreat across the river.

WARGAMING THE EBRO OFFENSIVE

The Ebro offensive offers a number of scenarios for wargames large and small, with the initial Republican offensive providing the most interest as a purely military operation. In a wider context, the war lends itself to multiplayer treatments covering both the military and political aspects.

In early 1937 General Franco explained his strategic method to Roberto Cantalupo, the Italian ambassador. He abjured the sort of lightning offensives proposed by Mola and by his German and Italian allies, favouring instead a 'town by town' approach. 'I am not interested in territory, but in inhabitants', he stated. He accepted that this was no recipe for martial glory and that it would prolong the war. Seldom has the primacy of political objectives in a military campaign been made more explicit, and if you are wargaming the Ebro operation as a whole, Franco's strategy is pivotal. He was not seeking a rapid military victory, rather a 'war of redemption' in which his enemies would be exterminated.

As we have seen, the consequences at the front line were grim for the soldiers of both sides. Franco had something like a million men under

A war memorial dedicated to the Nationalist 4th Navarrese Division, who took severe casualties in the Sierra de Pandols. This monument lies at the side of the road N230 south of Gandesa. (Author's photograph)

arms and could afford to be as profligate with their lives as an oriental despot. Once their own offensive had run its course, the Republicans had to hang on, hoping for a change in the international situation even if the military balance in Spain was tipping irrevocably against them. The stage was set for a grinding battle of attrition.

USING MINIATURES

Until recently, wargaming the Spanish Civil War with miniatures meant converting figures from other ranges. I used 20mm plastic figures, not just because they are cheap, but because they are easier to slice about. Matchbox and Airfix World War II British Commandos can have their woollen headgear chopped into *gorillos* (caps); old Airfix Germans had rather poorly moulded helmets that looked sufficiently Spanish to get away with, and Airfix once made Italian infantry too. I used aircraft fitters, World War I gunners, Luftwaffe ground crew and other characters in shirtsleeves to make up the numbers. Caps and berets are easily added with two-part epoxy metal filler intended for fixing rusty drainpipes. The uniform detail, and much inspiration, came from Jeffrey Burn's plates in the 1978 Men-at-Arms title 74 *The Spanish Civil War 1936–39* by Patrick Turnball.

Field guns were converted from the 13-pdr in the old Airfix World War I Royal Horse Artillery set. The sort of improvised armoured vehicles of the early war period were made just like the originals: take a toy bulldozer and add enough plasticard, cardboard and metal filler to give the right shape; fix a machine-gun or two and daub the vehicle with trade union acronyms and/or political slogans. Plastic tank kits are available for the PzKpfw I and Renault FT17 in 1:72 scale. The T-26 and BT-7 are made by the German company Minitanks, albeit in 1:87 scale; both Soviet tanks and the Italian CV33 tankette are sold by resin kit specialists in Britain, Australia and America. An international listing is carried by the website Storto@pilot.msu.edu. Since internet sites are ephemeral creatures, if that does not work, type 'Airfix' into any popular search engine and take it from there.

Some of these options are rather harder these days, with Airfix's decision to cease production of toy soldiers, but the moulds are up for sale, or licensed production, so one hopes they will not vanish. By way of compensation, Irregular's 'really useful gun range' includes most Spanish Civil War artillery in 15mm/20mm scale and Irregular's 1:300 scale Civil War figures are outstanding. There are fine ranges of figures available in metal 15mm and 20mm.

So much for the 'hardware'. What about the game mechanisms?

The Ebro offensive was on such a scale that the best way to wargame the whole operation is with the sort of systems pioneered by some members of 'Wargames Developments'. A couple of figures on a base represent a battalion or a weapons company; a single vehicle on a base represents a company or battalion. Magnetic tape stuck on the back of the base serves to secure strength marker counters cut from 'steel paper'. Only the owner of the unit knows its strength until the moment of combat, thus introducing an essential element of 'fog of war'. A groundscale of 1:2500 (40mm = 1km) will enable you to cover the entire operational area without hiring a ballroom for the game. At this scale, logistic considerations should loom large: although the Nationalists were able to

A monument to the Guardia Civil killed on the Ebro in Tortosa. In Spain most of the monuments are dedicated to Nationalist casualties and it is very rare to see one dedicated to Republican troops. In Britain Republican memorials have been dedicated to International Brigade troops, one such example has been erected in Jubilee Gardens near Waterloo Station in London. (Author's photograph)

deliver some fearsome bombardments as their counter-attacks progressed, the rhythm of the fighting was often affected by munitions shortages, especially on the Republican side.

The initial Republican offensive has the makings of an excellent operational game. The defence of a river line is frequently attempted in war, but, as Clausewitz observed, the theoretical defensive advantages rarely apply in practice. The attackers usually get across in sufficient numbers to survive any immediate counter-stroke: and in the case of the Ebro campaign, the crossing succeeded despite the Nationalists' air superiority and their capacity to raise the water level. You can also experiment with the sort of counter-attack strategies Franco rejected, like a pincer movement to sever the base of the bridgehead, instead of a Verdun-style 'meatgrinder'.

At battalion level, you are stuck with the strategies adopted historically. Two game systems, both developed for 1914-18, can be adapted for the Ebro offensive. The acquisition of intelligence through prisoner capture was pursued by Nationalists and Republicans alike, so a 'trench raid' across the lines offers a small-scale game ideal for an evening when time is at a premium. This can be scaled up to a company or battalion assault, ideally with two or three players commanding the attack and the defenders being operated by an umpire. This allows for far more realistic levels of confusion than a conventional 'face-to-face' wargame. A company or battalion attack can make a good solo game too, with the defences occupied by randomly generated enemy, modified by die rolls for the effectiveness of the initial artillery bombardment and/or air attack. I use an area movement system in a game simulating the US amphibious assaults in the Pacific. The Japanese defenders are represented by counters that begin the game face down (with some blanks added for confusion) so the initial bombardment might be concentrated on the wrong areas. You turn them up as you encounter them, die rolls enabling them to mass for counter-attacks. A similar system could be used to simulate the Nationalist assaults on Republican strongpoints.

I use a figure scale of 1 figure to 3 or 4 men and a groundscale of 1:1000 (100mm = 100m) for battalion-level actions in this period. The initial Republican attack makes for more fluid and exciting battles. The attacking forces included tanks, but they are primitive by World War II standards and few and far between. Artillery is not so concentrated as to constitute the sort of battering ram available on most European fronts in

One of the main reasons for the Republican defeat on the Ebro. The bomb loads of the Condor Legion and the Reggia Aeronautica, which acted as aerial artillery in conjunction Nationalist air units, caused havoc amongst supply lines and defensive positions. (Author's photograph)

1939-45. By the same token, airpower is relatively moderate in its impact. However, the same low ratios of artillery pieces to riflemen, and gunnery techniques primitive by the standards of 1917-18, make the Nationalist counter-attacks more like those of 1915 than 1939-45. Reconnaissance was often poor and objectives predictable. As noted above, the veterans of the Army of Africa were much depleted, their poorly trained replacements lacking their skill if not their enthusiasm. This is not the most promising combination for a tactical wargame.

A better bet at tactical level are the early war actions as Nationalist columns attempted to relieve citadels like Toledo, where rebel forces were besieged by loyalist troops and militias. These can be conventional games or, better, run with the players all on one side, 'road movie' style, with random or pre-planned 'events' to add to the fun. This is perhaps the most suitable option too for a solo game: you leading a column across a table with randomly generated dice-driven Republican forces. At that time the government's defenders were at their most disunited, with rival militias divided on regional or political lines and sometimes as antagonistic towards each other as to the Nationalists. Since these political divisions were at the heart of the conflict, they surely deserve games in their own right, to complement the more purely military ones outlined above.

STRATEGIC, POLITICAL, ROLE-PLAYING AND OTHER GAMES

The Spanish Civil War involved many factions, each with different (although not always mutually exclusive) objectives. At a 'Wargames Developments' conference a few years ago the complexities of the political situation were starkly illustrated in a multi-player game using the 'Matrix' game format pioneered by Chris Engle in the USA. As the technique requires only one person (the umpire) to have a thorough grounding in the period, it is a useful way of introducing people to a new military or political era without getting bogged down in learning lots of rules. Players take turns to advance an argument: you state an action, its consequence, and three reasons why it should occur. For instance: my Republican division attacks across the Ebro, with the result that the Nationalist defence in this sector is completely broken. This will happen because (a) the Republican troops are well trained, (b) we have prepared and rehearsed our river crossing techniques, and (c) the Nationalist defences are thinly stretched. The umpire rolls a die, allowing 'good' arguments to succeed most of the time and 'poor' arguments only on a good score. The exact odds depend on how you like to play the game. I use a D10 and allot a 10-90 per cent chance of success according to the ingenuity of the arguments. An argument that directly contradicts a previously successful argument has a sharply reduced chance of success (I allow no more than 20 per cent). A more stylish alternative is to turn someone's argument against them, e.g. your opponent argues his Nationalist column force-marches to stop the Republican advance, you counter with an ambush, arguing that the enemy do indeed make fast progress, but neglect basic security precautions in their haste.

The 'Matrix' technique is not to everyone's taste, and some critics regard it as little more than 'Mornington Crescent' with soldiers, but as demonstration games have shown at recent UK wargames conventions, it can provide an entertaining and informative game with no preparation demanded of the players. It is especially suited to a subject like the Spanish Civil War with its multitude of belligerent groups, each with several objectives. It highlights the political divisions within the Nationalist and Republican camps, and the danger of factions breaking away. After all, with greater subtlety, Franco might have detached the Basques from the republic; instead, his policy of revenge and repression helped fuel the separatist movement that still plagues the Spanish state. Franco's transformation from leading general to unassailable dictator could even become a game in itself: a Machiavellian rise to power in which he outwitted able leaders like Gil Robles as well as the new head of the Falange, Manuel Hedilla.

The Ebro offensive signalled the beginning of the end for the republic, which generated a new round of infighting between government factions. The spectacle of Negrín's government urging everyone to fight on to the last while the leaders arranged their flights to safety abroad eventually sparked a mutiny. In Madrid, Colonel Casado led a rising against the regime, hoping that Franco might agree to a negotiated settlement. There was a revolt at the naval base of Cartagena, aided by Franco's agents and quashed just ahead of an amphibious landing by Nationalist forces. Both episodes are suitable subjects for the 'Matrix' game treatment, or more conventional role-playing games in which the players have three or four objectives kept secret from the others.

GLOSSARY

Tabor	Half Battalion
Regulares	Native infantry
Bandera/s	Battalion
Tercio	Regiment
Teniente	Lieutenant
Commandante	Commandant
Coronel	Colonel
Teniente Coronel	Lieutenant Colonel
Capitán	Captain
Sargento	Sergeant
Grupo	Regiment
Cabo	Corporal
Sub-Oficial	NCO
Agrupación	Artillery brigade/*ad hoc* unit
Brigada Mixta	Mixed Brigade
Alferez	Junior Lieutenant
Mayor	Major
Oficial	Officer
Estado Mayor	General Staff
Jefe de Estado Mayor	Chief of Staff
Oficial de Enlace	Liason Officer
Puesto de Mando	Command Post

FURTHER READING

As far as the author is aware there are no English language publications that deal specifically with the Ebro campaign. Everything else is written in Spanish. The following are a list of works consulted during the preparation of this book.

Alpert, M., *El Ejército de la Republica en la Guerra Civil* (Barcelona, 1978)

Armero, J.M., *Armas Y Pertrechos de La Guerra Civil de España* (Madrid, 1982)

Aznar, M., *Historia militar de la Guerra de España* (Madrid, 1958)

Ballester, R., *La Batalla del Ebro* (Barcelona, 1974)

Bender, R.J., *Uniforms Organization and History of the Condor Legion* (San José, 1992)

Frazer, R., *Blood of Spain* (London, 1986)

Garbate Cordoba, J.M., *Partes Oficiales de Guerra 1936–39* (Madrid, 1978)

Hernandez, J., *Yo Ministro de Stalin en España* (Madrid, 1954)

Kindelán, A., *Mis Cuadernos de Guerra* (Madrid)

Larios, J., *Combat over Spain* (London, 1971)

Líster, E., *Memorias de un Luchador* (Barcelona, 1977)

Llarch, J., *La Batalla del Ebro* (Barcelona-Valencia, 1972)

Martínez Bande, J.M., *La Batalla del Ebro* (Madrid, 1988)

Martínez de Campos, C., *Dos Batallas de La Guerra de Liberación de España* (Madrid, 1962)

Mezquida y Gené, L.M., *La Batalla del Ebro* (Taragona, 1967).

Modesto, J., *Soy del Quinto Regimiento* (Paris, 1969)

Mortera Perez, A. and Infiesta Perez, J.L., *La Artillería en La Guerra Civil, Material de Origen Italiano importado por el Ejercito Nacional* (Valladolid, 1997)

Mortera Perez, A. and Infiesta Perez, J.L., *La Artillería en La Guerra Civil, Material de Origen Aleman importado por el Ejercito Nacional* (Valladolid, 1996)

Rojo, V., *España Heroica* (Buenos Aires, 1942)

Salas Larrazabal, J., *Intervención en la Guerra Civil* (Barcelona,1974)

Salas Larrazabal, J., *La Guerra de España desde el Aire* (Barcelona, 1969)

Salas Larrazabal, R., *La Historía del Ejército Popular de la República* (Madrid, 1973)

Sweet, J.J.T., *Iron Arm: The Mechanization of Mussolini's Army* (Conneticut, 1980)

Tagüeña Lacorte, M., *Testimonio de Dos Guerras* (Mexico, 1974)

Tarazona, F., *Yo fui piloto de caza rojo* (Madrid, 1968)

Thomas, H., *The Spanish Civil War* (Harmondsworth, 1977)

Primary Sources:

Servicio Historico Militar, Avila.

Hermeroteca Bilbao.

Foreign Office Archives PRO, Kew.

INDEX

Figures in **bold** refer to illustrations